PRAISE FOR *JONATHAN EDWARDS ON GENESIS*

"This fine study not only reflects recent trends in Edwards studies but offers a fresh look at previously unpublished sources in the Edwardsean corpus. With his eyes set firmly on pastor-scholar sensibilities, Borgman provides a lucid account of Jonathan Edwards as an exegete of the book of Genesis and explains how Edwards as a pastor underpinned his exegetical sermons as well as other writings. This volume will benefit readers of various stripes both in the church and in the academy."

—CHRIS CHUN, director of Jonathan Edwards Center and professor, Gateway Seminary

"It has been rightly said that the history of the church is the story of the church's interaction with the Bible, and one of the most influential figures in this story was the New England divine Jonathan Edwards. In recent years, his role in the reception history of the Scriptures has proven to be an especially fruitful subject of historical enquiry. This new monograph on his reflections on the book of Genesis continues and sharpens this inquiry, and reveals the way that Edwards was both a faithful transmitter of previous exegesis and a pioneer in new paths of thinking."

—MICHAEL A.G. HAYKIN, The Southern Baptist Theological Seminary

"This study adds to the growing body of literature that considers Edwards as an exegete, and helpfully focuses our attention on his exposition of texts from the book of Genesis, which, with its accounts of creation and the fall, was a major object of examination in the early modern period. Here, then, we see Edwards as a participant in a community of students of the Bible. But we also see his unique employment of that study, not only in his reflections on specific passages, but also for developing vital loci such as the *imago Dei*, or image of God. Even more, we are treated here to the connection between Edwards's exposition and his preaching, showing the intimate relation these pursuits had for him and the way they informed each other."

—KENNETH P. MINKEMA, Jonathan Edwards Center, Yale University

"As the author of a theological commentary on Genesis, I was eager to learn how Jonathan Edwards, one of my favorite theologians, interacted with the first book of Moses. Borgman's monograph did not disappoint. His analysis allowed me to peek over Edwards's shoulder in the study and to feel his pathos in the pulpit. I gained a deeper appreciation for Edwards's sensitivity to the typological layers of the text and his burden to apply the Word to his parishioners. If you're a fan of the Great Awakening preacher and New England's premiere theologian, I recommend Borgman's helpful treatment."

—ROBERT GONZALES JR., author of *Where Sin Abounds: The Spread of Sin and the Curse in Genesis*

Jonathan Edwards on Genesis

Jonathan Edwards on Genesis

Hermeneutics, Homiletics, and Theology

BRIAN BORGMAN

Foreword by Adriaan C. Neele

WIPF & STOCK · Eugene, Oregon

JONATHAN EDWARDS ON GENESIS
Hermeneutics, Homiletics, and Theology

Copyright © 2021 Brian Borgman. All rights reserved. Except for brief quotations in critical publications or reviews, no part of this book may be reproduced in any manner without prior written permission from the publisher. Write: Permissions, Wipf and Stock Publishers, 199 W. 8th Ave., Suite 3, Eugene, OR 97401.

Wipf & Stock
An Imprint of Wipf and Stock Publishers
199 W. 8th Ave., Suite 3
Eugene, OR 97401

www.wipfandstock.com

PAPERBACK ISBN: 978-1-6667-0577-5
HARDCOVER ISBN: 978-1-6667-0578-2
EBOOK ISBN: 978-1-6667-0579-9

07/07/21

To Ashley Grace Feathers,
our precious daughter, who is a blessing and source of joy to us.
I love you and am so thankful to be your dad.

Contents

Foreword by Adriaan C. Neele	xi
Acknowledgments	xiii
Abstract	xv
Author's Note	xvii
Chapter One Introduction: The Edwards "Renaissance"	1
Chapter Two Edwards's Interpretive Tradition, the Enlightenment, and Critical Method	17

PART ONE: EXEGETICAL AND HOMILETICAL

Chapter Three Jonathan Edwards's Exegesis of Genesis: Genesis Sermons (1727–1735)	25
Chapter Four Jonathan Edwards's Exegesis of Genesis: Genesis Sermons (1736–1739)	42
Chapter Five Edwards's Use of Genesis in *A History of the Work of Redemption*	64

PART TWO: THEOLOGICAL

Chapter Six Edwards's Theology of Man in the Image of God	79
Conclusion and Prospect	108
Bibliography	113
Name Index	117
Scripture Index	119

Foreword

JONATHAN EDWARDS. THE NAME has become almost equal with New England's revival and Great Awakening of the eighteenth century. Since Perry Miller's revisionist view of the colonial Puritan theocracy, cultivated at Harvard University in the 1920s, and the research and critical edition of the *Works of Jonathan Edwards* at Yale University (1957—), the life and thought of Edwards has seen an unprecedented renaissance of scholarship: worldwide through the Yale-affiliated research centers in Australia, Belgium, Brazil, Germany, Hungary, Japan, Poland, and the United Kingdom, as well as on the West Coast and Midwest of America, besides the main center at Yale University, Connecticut.

The rise of publications on the life and work of Edwards has shown significant interest in his major works such as *A History of the Work of Redemption* (1739/1788), *A Treatise Concerning Religious Affections* (1746), *Life of David Brainerd* (1749), *Freedom of the Will* (1754), and "The End for Which God Created the World" (1765), among other works. Besides, secondary literature throughout the twentieth century has given attention to Edwards's theology, philosophy, missiology, history, revivalism, literature, and cultural criticism. But a recent and new development in Edwards studies is a sustained interest in Edwards's homiletics and biblical studies. Most recent scholarship suggests that sermons and the study of specific books of Scripture contribute in new and fresh ways for a more complete understanding of Edwards's intellectual and pastoral endeavors.

This study by Brian Borgman is a fine example of the most current research trends in Edwards scholarship—a study conducted and completed at the Jonathan Edwards Center Midwest at Puritan Reformed Theological Seminary, Michigan.

As such, this study stands out in *three* ways: this study is a *first* in scholarship on Edwards's use of the book of Genesis and adds to studies with a single focus on the Bible books Romans and Psalms, for example. *Second*, this study offers an interdisciplinary approach to reading Edwards: biblical exegesis, homiletics, and theology. The study suggests that Edwards's theology of man in the image of God benefits from his insights of exegesis and sermons. The latter, the sermons on Genesis, has been studied in its totality within Edwards's sermon corpus, and chronologically in the periods of 1727–1735 and 1736–1739. The use and appraisal of the Genesis-texts in the famous "Redemption Discourse" (1739) underscore the benefit of an interdisciplinary research approach. *Third*, this study does not only contribute to Edwards scholarship, the academy, but serves the church, as well, and demonstrates that Edwards's applicatory emphasis in his sermons revealed his pastoral heart for his congregation.

May this study be a benefit to those who study Edwards and a blessing to those seeking to be edified by Edwards's sermons.

Dr. Adriaan C. Neele
Jonathan Edwards Center Midwest at Puritan Reformed Theological Seminary

Acknowledgments

My love for Jonathan Edwards began as a seminary student. My church history professor, Dr. Bob Krupp, had us read original sources, and *Religious Affections* was on the reading list. John Piper fueled the journey in many ways. Over the years, I read Edwards and read about Edwards with great relish. Then I had the privilege of studying Edwards under Dr. Adriaan Neele, an extraordinary Edwards scholar.

I extend the warmest gratitude to my teachers over the years, who shaped me spiritually and theologically. During my Western Seminary days, I have a debt of gratitude to Jim Andrews (my professor and pastor), Dr. Duane Dunham, and Dr. Bruce Ware. During my Westminster days, I was deeply impacted by visiting lecturer Dr. Joel Beeke and my advisor, Dr. Joey Pipa. At Puritan Reformed Theological Seminary, I benefitted from Dr. Greg Salazar and Dr. Stephen Meyers. My special debt of gratitude is to Dr. Adriaan Neele, one of the most impressive scholars I have ever met. Dr. Neele's careful interaction and expert instruction will not be soon forgotten. Thank you, Dr. Neele, for writing the foreword.

Many thanks to Laura Ladwig, librarian extraordinaire. Megan Wilhelm helped me in immeasurable ways in preparing the manuscript. I am grateful.

Of course, my wife, Ariel, deserves much praise for putting up with me, especially during periods of research and writing. She is my best friend, and I thank God for her.

Abstract

PERRY MILLER (1905-1963) HAS often been credited with the resurgence of scholarly interest in Jonathan Edwards (1703-1758). Edwards and his writings have been studied from numerous angles. However, Edwards as an exegete is a recent area of research. Edwards was deeply committed to a high view of Scripture. The Bible was central for Edwards in every area of life. Indeed, he was a man immersed in the Bible as an avid student, interpreter, and preacher. With this recent focus on Edwards as an exegete, and narrower focus on Edwards's handling different genres and sections of Scripture, this study explores first Edwards's exegesis of the book of Genesis—an unexplored area in Edwards studies. Genesis played a significant part in Edwards's worldview, theology, and ministry. This study will examine Edwards's exegetical and homiletical approach to Genesis and explore the related Genesis theme of the image of God. Edwards's view of the image of God, which plays such a vital role in Genesis 1-2, was significant in his anthropology. The result of this research will be to contribute to the field of study on Edwards as an exegete of Holy Scripture, using Genesis and the related theme of the image of God.

Author's Note

A WORD ABOUT QUOTING Edwards: In the body of this work, any citation of a source that quotes Edwards will be left as it is in the quote. Any direct quotation from Edwards will slightly edit Edwards's shorthand, symbols, antiquated spellings, and punctuation.

Chapter One

Introduction

The Edwards "Renaissance"

"CURRENT SCHOLARLY INTEREST, A veritable Edwardsean 'Renaissance,' remains strong as it builds on seminal twentieth-century research and manuscript studies. There are healthy indications that attention to Edwards's life and thought will not ebb quickly." Thus said Helen Westra in 1986.[1] That interest in Edwards has not ebbed is attested by the growing number of publications and research centers.[2] Popular-level publications on Edwards have kept a steady and even an increasing pace.[3] Scholarly works also continue to

---

1. Westra, *Minister's Task and Calling*, i.

2. Lesser's *Reading Jonathan Edwards* extends to over six hundred pages. In 2013, *Jonathan Edwards Studies* 3, no. 1, produced "Recent Publications," which provided a non-comprehensive list of publications, from 2005 to 2012, twenty-five pages, single-spaced (*Jonathan Edwards Studies* 3, no. 1, 173–97.) A subsequent list has been released in 2014, 2015, 2016, and 2017. The Jonathan Edwards Center at Yale University has seventy-three volumes of Edwards's works online. From 1956 to 2008, there were twenty-six printed volumes and then the additional forty-seven volumes were added online (Edwards.yale.edu). It is not only Edwards's alma mater that has an Edwards Center, there are Edwards Centers in South Africa, Australia, Belgium, Netherlands, Luxembourg, Brazil, Germany, Hungary, Japan, Poland, and United Kingdom, as well as at Trinity Evangelical Divinity School in Deerfield, Illinois, and Gateway Seminary in Ontario, California (edwards.yale.edu/Global+centers).

3. The Banner of Truth Trust, Soli Deo Gloria (an imprint of Reformation Heritage Books), and other publishers have continued to produce uncritical reprints, which make healthy contributions to the Edwards Renaissance. The Banner of Truth Trust

be produced at a rapid rate.⁴ Kenneth P. Minkema, writing in 2004, notes, "The number of secondary publications on Edwards fast approaches 4,000, making him *the* most studied American intellectual figure before 1800."⁵ The ebb is nowhere in sight.

This interest in Edwards would have been surprising to many. Ezra Stiles (1727–1795), president of Yale, famously said of the works of Jonathan Edwards that they "in another generation will pass into as transient notice perhaps scarce above oblivion, and when posterity occasionally comes across them in the rubbish of libraries, the rare characters who may read them will be looked upon as singular and whimsical."⁶ Stiles was almost correct for a time. Edwards was neglected for a while, but many Edwards scholars point to Perry Miller and his biography of Edwards in 1949 as a turning point in interest in Edwards. "Miller's biography marked the beginning of a significant scholarly renaissance among historians, theologians, and philosophers interested in Edwards's life and thought."⁷

Edwards's biographer George Marsden notes in the foreword to *The Jonathan Edwards Encyclopedia*,

> This work is published at a very appropriate time, for during the past couple of generations there has been a remarkable revival

---

reprints of the two-volume Hickman edition of *The Works of Jonathan Edwards*, as well as collections of sermons, works on revival, and Brainerd's dairy, have sold well. Additionally, Iain Murray's biography, *Jonathan Edwards: A New Biography*, and other secondary literature have helped introduce Edwards at a popular level. Soli Deo Gloria has published many volumes of Edwards's sermons. Secondary popular-level literature on Edwards has also grown rapidly. Authors like John Gerstner, John Piper, Sam Storms, Stephen Nichols, Steven Lawson, Douglas Sweeney, and Owen Strachan have all made major contributions to popular secondary literature.

4. There are volumes of never-before-published sermons being transcribed and edited and put into print, such as *Sermons by Jonathan Edwards on the Matthean Parables*, 3 vols., ed. Minkema, Neele, and McCarthy; "reader" volumes have also been produced, introducing Edwards's sermons (*The Sermons of Jonathan Edwards: A Reader*, Kimnach et al.) and major writings (*A Reader's Guide to the Major Writings of Jonathan Edwards*, Finn and Kimble). There was also George Marsden's landmark biography on the tricentennial of Edwards's birth, *Jonathan Edwards: A Life*; *The Princeton Companion to Jonathan Edwards*; *The Cambridge Companion to Jonathan Edwards*; McClymond's and McDermott's, *The Theology of Jonathan Edwards*; and *The Jonathan Edwards Encyclopedia*. The JESociety Press in 2017 launched a series "given exclusively to the select publication of cutting-edge research related to America's greatest theologian" (available through jesociety.org).

5. Minkema, "Jonathan Edwards in the Twentieth Century," 678. Minkema's article details the growth of academic literature on Edwards in the twentieth century under eight different categories of study.

6. Quoted in Marsden, *Jonathan Edwards: A Life*, 498–99.

7. Finn and Kimble, *Reader's Guide*, 17.

of interest in Edwards. Edwards had been highly regarded, especially in New England, for a couple generations after his death. But then he fell out of style. By the early twentieth century he was known chiefly for *Sinners in the Hands of an Angry God* and was regarded in leading intellectual and theological circles as, even if a genius, primarily a representative of the harsh theology that American Christians should be getting beyond. By the mid-twentieth century he had few professed followers.[8]

Edwards studies are multidimensional and multifaceted. As Westra commented, "Scholars have written prolifically on Edwards's revivalist activities, his sulfurous sermons, and his sinewy thought, the complexity and range of his mind in multifarious studies and bibliographic entries on Edwards as philosopher, scientist, theologian, ethicist, logician, typologist, psychologist, proto-romanticist, revivalist, historian, mystic, and literary artist."[9] But one area that seems to have not garnered much attention over the years is Edwards as an exegete, interpreter, and expositor of Holy Scripture.[10] This is interesting since Edwards was first and foremost a man of the Bible. Edwards's life was devoted to and shaped by studying the Scriptures and preaching the Scriptures. In Resolution 28 Edwards wrote, "Resolved, to study the Scriptures so steadily, constantly and frequently, as that I may find, and plainly perceive myself to grow in the knowledge of the same."[11] Edwards, also noted in his diary in 1723,

> I had then, and at other times, the greatest delight in the holy Scriptures, of any book whatsoever. Oftentimes in reading it, every word seemed to touch my heart. I felt a harmony between something in my heart, and those sweet and powerful words. I seemed often to see so much light, exhibited by every sentence, and such a refreshing ravishing food communicated, that I could not get along in reading. Used oftentimes to dwell long on one sentence, to see the wonders contained in it; and yet almost every sentence seemed to be full of wonders.[12]

---

8. Marsden, foreword to Stout et al., *The Jonathan Edwards Encyclopedia*, vi–vii.

9. Westra, *Minister's Task and Calling*, iii.

10. This trend is being reversed, as will be documented shortly, with such works as Barshinger's *Jonathan Edwards and the Psalms* and Sweeney's *Edwards the Exegete*.

11. *The Works of Jonathan Edwards* (hereafter *WJE*), 16:755.

12. *WJE* 16:797.

RECENT SCHOLARSHIP ON EDWARDS AS BIBLICAL INTERPRETER

If Edwards's love and devotion to Scripture were so central to his thought and life, calling and ministry, why has it been so neglected? David P. Barshinger addresses this:

> But despite his acknowledged place in American religious history—not to mention the broader history of Christianity—the role of the Bible in his thought has rarely received the attention it deserves. Yet Edwards clearly stood in the stream of *sola scriptura*, and Scripture had a formative influence on his thought, which, if ignored, can skew our understanding of the man.[13]

Douglas Sweeney makes a similar observation:

> Three hundred years after his birth, half a century into what some have called the Edwards renaissance, few have bothered to study Edwards's massive exegetical corpus. While preoccupied with his place in America's public life and letters—and failing to see the public significance of his biblical exegesis—we have ignored the scholarly work he took most seriously.[14]

The historian and the theologian must be able to "see things their way."[15] To "see things their way" is to understand and present the times and the thoughts of a historical figure in a way that the historical figure could recognize them as his own.[16] To downplay or even ignore the role of the Bible in Edwards's thought and life would be to create a portrait of Edwards that would be, at best, incomplete. Considering his exceptional devotion and assiduous attention to the Bible, as revealed through his exegetical reflections, sermons, and commentary, "oversight of the importance of the Bible to Edwards has kept us from the true Jonathan Edwards."[17] As Barshinger points out, it is not enough to simply assume the Bible played a role in Edwards's life because of the culture in which Edwards lived.[18] Virtually everything in Edwards thought and life was shaped by his study of the

---

13. Barshinger, introduction to *Jonathan Edwards and Scripture*, ed. Barshinger and Sweeney, 1.

14. Sweeney, *Edwards the Exegete*, 7.

15. Chapman et al. *Seeing Things Their Way*.

16. Gregory, "Can We 'See Things Their Way'? Should We Try?," in Chapman et al., *Seeing Things Their Way*, 27.

17. Nichols, *Jonathan Edwards's Bible*, 1.

18. Barshinger, introduction to *Jonathan Edwards and Scripture*, ed. Barshinger and Sweeney, 2.

Bible. This central driving force of Edwards's thought and life is, however, currently being explored with more interest.[19]

Douglas A. Sweeney wrote in 2009, "I am compelled by Edwards's devotion to the reality of the divine, the divinity of the Bible, and the Bible's importance for life, that I have found myself attempting to make it contagious."[20] Sweeney's desire to make Edwards's love for the Bible contagious was realized in David P. Barshinger, who studied under Sweeney at Trinity Evangelical Divinity School. Barshinger's work is the fruit of his doctoral studies, which were supervised by Sweeney. *Jonathan Edwards and the Psalms: A Redemptive-Historical Vision of Scripture* is one of the most significant studies in this field, and it focuses on a specific area of the canon, namely, the Psalms.

Barshinger focuses on Edwards's use of the Psalms for a variety of reasons. First, if Edwards on Scripture has been generally ignored, then almost certainly, his engagement with the Psalms would also have been ignored. "As for Edwards's work on the Psalms, no monograph, journal article, or essay has been devoted to this topic."[21] Furthermore, the Psalms played a significant role in the worship and theology of the church. Singing the Psalms, especially in Edwards's New England, was formative for the lives of the congregations. But more importantly, as Barshinger notes, "Edwards himself found the Psalms to be rich with theological depth and spiritual enrichment, and he used this book extensively and substantively in his writings and ministry."[22] Barshinger notes that Edwards cited the Psalms more than any other book of the Bible in the twenty-six printed volumes of the Yale *Works of Jonathan Edwards*.[23] It is clear from the "Blank Bible," "Notes on Scripture," and Edwards's sermons, that "Edwards had a special affinity

---

19. A significant figure in reviving Edwards as a man devoted to Scripture is Stephen J. Stein. Stein has not only edited several editions of the *Works of Jonathan Edwards*, he has edited the volumes which demonstrate Edwards's most vigorous interaction with the Bible: *Apocalyptic Writings*, vol. 5; "Notes on Scripture," vol. 15; and the "Blank Bible," vol. 24. Stein's introductions emphasize Edwards as an exegete. Stein notes, "The publication of the Yale Edition of the *Works* has further stimulated this expanding interest in and growing knowledge of Edwards's exegetical writings. Several volumes already published in the Edition shed considerable light on the scriptural side of his thought. This volume will make possible more sophisticated study of his biblical exegesis. Future volumes promise to provide access to his other exegetical texts" (*WJE*, "Notes on Scripture," Stein, 15:34).

20. Sweeney, *Jonathan Edwards and the Ministry of the Word*, 21.

21. Barshinger, *Jonathan Edwards and the Psalms*, 21.

22. Barshinger, *Jonathan Edwards and the Psalms*, 6.

23. Barshinger, *Jonathan Edwards and the Psalms*, 6.

for the Psalms."[24] This special affinity was not merely ministerial, but it was also deeply personal. "Edwards made the sweetness of the Psalms his 'own language,' and this study probes what was in the Psalms that appeared so 'excellent' and 'sweet' to this learned New England divine."[25]

Barshinger explores Edwards's "theological engagement with the Psalms not only to help correct the distorted picture of Edwards that leaves out his biblicism but also to describe the details of how his commitment to Scripture colored his life and thought."[26] Barshinger organizes his book around major theological themes, the doctrine of God and the Word, man and sin, Christology, the Spirit and the gospel, Christian piety, and the church and eternity. Each topic is developed through Edwards's use of the Psalms as they relate to these topics.

Barshinger constantly keeps in view Edwards's own emphasis on the history of redemption. The history of redemption was of course near and dear to Edwards. Barshinger acknowledges that Edwards's interpretive approach to any given psalm is hardly monolithic, however, it is held together by a larger perspective which Barshinger calls, "redemptive-historical." Barshinger summarizes, "My thesis is that in a world experiencing major epistemological shorts and liturgical challenges, Jonathan Edwards appropriated the book of Psalms as a divinely inspired anchor to proclaim the gospel and rehearse the redemptive-historical work of the triune God."[27] Barshinger concludes, "Any discussion of Edwards's theology must incorporate the concept of the history of redemption."[28]

Barshinger views Edwards as a biblicist, with strong pre-critical convictions, but who was also very much aware of the Enlightenment and critical thought and methodology. Any employment of critical method was to serve a deeper understanding of the history of redemption. Neither the Enlightenment or critical methodology moved Edwards from his commitment to the divine nature of Scripture, rather, he interacted with it apologetically and used it to further his studies. Furthermore, Edwards's commitment to pre-critical exegesis was not, as Barshinger notes, a commitment to medieval Catholic quadriga, but rather to a Protestant and Puritan tradition of typology. Granted, Edwards pushed typology further than some, but always within his reliance on the analogy of the faith and the analogy of Scripture.[29]

---

24. Barshinger, *Jonathan Edwards and the Psalms*, 9.
25. Barshinger, *Jonathan Edwards and the Psalms*, 14.
26. Barshinger, *Jonathan Edwards and the Psalms*, 26.
27. Barshinger, *Jonathan Edwards and the Psalms*, 26.
28. Barshinger, *Jonathan Edwards and the Psalms*, 360.
29. Barshinger, *Jonathan Edwards and the Psalms*, 366. Barshinger points out that

Barshinger summarizes,

> Looking for a single category for Edwards from our categories today misleads us away from capturing the complexity of his exegesis of the Psalms day by day as he studied the Bible, prepared sermons, worshiped with his congregation and in private, nurtured his own spiritual life, and ministered pastorally to others. . . . So he fluidly used grammatical-historical, scriptural-analogical, typological, Christological, ecclesiological, devotional, and theological methods of interpretation, but the organizing framework that governed his interpretation of the Psalms as he employed these diverse methods was the triune God's work of redemption in history.[30]

In 2016, Douglas Sweeney published *Edwards the Exegete*, which was a rigorous scholarly effort in setting forth the role of Scripture in Edwards's thought, life, and ministry.

Sweeney's work is divided into five parts. Part 1, "Prolegomena," is devoted to "The Biblical World of Jonathan Edwards" and "The Character of Scripture." Sweeney examines Edwards's commitment to Scripture and his doctrine of Scripture. Sweeney notes that "Edwards devoted most of his waking life to studying the Bible, its extra-biblical contexts, its theological meanings, and its import for everyday religion."[31] After exposing some reasons for neglecting this aspect of Edwards, Sweeney then makes the case that serious attention must be given to how Edwards studied Scripture, what tools he used, and why he studied the specific areas he did. There is no shortage of material here, in large part, because of the way Edwards studied. Edwards not only left a huge body of sermonic literature, but his "Blank Bible" and "Notes on Scripture" reflect his study habit of pen in hand, building on his thoughts over years.

Sweeney explores Edwards's resources for studying the Scriptures, including the biblical languages, Bible commentaries, and even textual criticism. Edwards gave himself whole-heartedly to the study of Scripture and anything he thought would help him understand Scripture. Everything was subservient to Scripture, and therefore, Edwards was not locked into reading in only one tradition or drinking at only one well of theology. Sweeney helpfully summarizes Edwards, "He was a 'both-and' thinker: traditional and modern, partisan and ecumenical, critical and edifying, catholic and anti-Catholic."[32]

---

this is Stephen R. C. Nichols's argument in *Jonathan Edwards and the Bible*.

30. Barshinger, *Jonathan Edwards and the Psalms*, 368.
31. Sweeney, *Edwards the Exegete*, 5.
32. Sweeney, *Edwards the Exegete*, 20.

Sweeney expounds on Edwards's convictions about the nature of Scripture in the second chapter, "The Character of Scripture." Again, it is crucial not to assume what Edwards believed about the Bible, but to explicitly state it. "Edwards believed in his bones that the Bible was divine."[33] Edwards's perspective on the divine inspiration of the Bible put him strongly in the Calvinistic tradition that the Scriptures were "self-authenticating," that is, the intrinsic nature of Scripture, its inherent power and sweetness, are its own best testimony to its divine origin. However, Edwards did not discount external evidence, such as prophecies and miracles. But for Edwards nothing surpassed the internal evidence. Sweeney, quoting Edwards, states,

> "The child of God doth . . . see and feel the truth of divine things," he said. The saints 'can feel such a power and kind of omnipotency in Christianity, and taste such a sweetness, and see such wisdom, such as excellent harmony in the gospel, as carry their own light with them, and powerfully do enforce and conquer the assent and necessitates their minds to receive it as proceeding from God, and as the certain truth."[34]

For Edwards, when the Word is preached, people should tremble at the Word, either with fear or with delight. The power of the Word preached does not spring primarily from what is remembered from the sermon, as much as it is from the impression made on the heart and mind at the time of preaching. The auditor encounters God through the preaching of the Word. There is powerful illumination by the Spirit through the Word. This illumination is spiritual knowledge, but spiritual knowledge must be based on natural or notional knowledge; in other words, both the regenerate and unregenerate must think before they can see or taste the sweetness of the Word. Such sight and taste are the work of the Holy Spirit. Laboring in the Word is what gives understanding and light. The Spirit's power is what gives spiritual understanding, or taste and heat.

Sweeney presents Edwards the exegete from multiple perspectives. Sweeney lays out how Edwards understood the principles of biblical interpretation and exegesis. This will be an important topic picked up later, but, as Sweeney points out, Edwards was very much at home interpreting the Bible literally and spiritually. "Edwards stands as a typical Reformed scholar of the early-modern period."[35] This is a significant part of Sweeney's book and in many ways lays the foundation for what he is going to explore regarding Edwards the exegete. Sweeney importantly states,

33. Sweeney, *Edwards the Exegete*, 28.
34. Sweeney, *Edwards the Exegete*, 31.
35. Sweeney, *Edwards the Exegete*, 48.

Edwards did things with the Bible few would do today. His theological exegesis fails to meet our modern standards of grammatical, historical, and scientific rigor. He was not a commentator in the usual sense of the word. Nor did he labor as a scholar in the field of ancient history. He studied what he deemed to be the very Word of God as a congregational minister and Christian theologian. He was biased in its favor. He believed that it cohered. And he read and spoke about it as a matter of life and death. Further, as Stein has emphasized, he sometimes "celebrated the violence at the heart of the biblical accounts," applying it in ways that can offend more peaceable Christians. He cheered the spread of the gospel through the rise and fall of nations. He believed that God is glorified when sinners go to hell. He would not pass muster in our leading universities.[36]

Sweeney goes on in the remainder of his book to show Edwards's commitment to canonical exegesis, christological exegesis, redemptive-historical exegesis, which includes his eschatological view, and finally, exegesis that results in practical knowledge, or, divinity, that is, "the doctrine of living to God by Christ."[37] For Edwards, the canon of Scripture provides the authoritative principles of the "analogy of Scripture," where the interpreter compares texts with texts and interprets Scripture with Scripture; and the "analogy of faith," where there is a doctrinal core that forms a doctrinal standard by which the interpreter tests his exegesis. Edwards was a doctrinal or theological interpreter.

Edwards also understood the Bible covenantally. The unifying theme of Scripture was the Trinitarian covenant of redemption, covenant of works, and covenant of grace. The Bible's harmony with itself was beautiful (beauty is a major theme in Edwards's thought). So much of Edwards's work in the Scriptures was making these harmonious connections between the testaments and between individual texts. This harmony was seen by Edwards most clearly in typology. This is a rich field of labor and will be revisited as Edwards on Genesis is investigated.

This harmony of the canon was preeminently christological. "For Edwards, Christ stood at the center of God's purpose in the creation and redemption of the world—a kind of cosmic keystone or, better, an infinite source of love binding the universe together. God did everything ad extra through His Son, for His Son, to secure a creaturely object of divine love for His Son."[38] This christological harmony is nowhere more fully displayed

---

36. Sweeney, *Edwards the Exegete*, 48.
37. Sweeney, *Edwards the Exegete*, 197.
38. Sweeney, *Edwards the Exegete*, 97.

than in redemptive history. If Christ is the harmonizing center of Scripture, the history of redemption is the vehicle to convey it.

Finally, for Edwards, Christian knowledge was for living to God through Christ. Nothing in Edwards's understanding of Scripture was merely theoretical; it was all practical. As referenced earlier, Edwards saw divinity in explicitly practical terms. Sweeney quotes Edwards at length:

> Divinity is commonly defined, *the doctrine of living to God*; and by some who seem to be more accurate, *the doctrine of living to God by Christ*.[39] It comprehends all Christian doctrines as they are in Jesus, and all Christian rules directing us in living to God by Christ. There is no divinity, no one doctrine, no promise, no rule, but what some way or other relates to the Christian and divine life, or our living to God by Christ. They all relate to this, in two respects, viz. as they tend to promote our living to God here in this world, in a life of faith and holiness, and also as they tend to bring us to a life of perfect holiness and happiness, in the full enjoyment of God hereafter.[40]

Sweeney's work puts Edwards into perspective, clearly demonstrating Edwards's devotion to the Scriptures as the source of wisdom, knowledge, and life. Without seeing Edwards in the context of what he did for hours every day of his life, assiduously studying Scripture, is not to see Edwards correctly. Edwards's convictions about the nature and function of Scripture, as well as his commitments to exegetical method, is to see Edwards as he would have seen himself. Sweeney's significant contribution to Edwards as exegete is that he does not put Edwards into one interpretive category, he shows how Edwards was multifaceted in his approach to Scripture, within broader historical-grammatical, christological, typological, and redemptive-historical frameworks. Sweeney's work has been deeply influential and has led to some other academic endeavors to understand how Edwards handled certain portions of Scripture.

David S. Lovi and Benjamin Westerhoff, in 2013, took up the task of compiling Edwards's comments on the book of Romans, *The Power of God: A Jonathan Edwards Commentary on the Book of Romans*. A task, which according to Sweeney in the foreword, was first assigned to John Gerstner by Perry Miller, but never came to fruition. Lovi and Westerhoff, inspired by Gerstner, and no doubt, Sweeney, compiled this "commentary." The project

---

39. This phrase comes from Ramus, Perkins, Ames, and is then expanded by Edwards's favorite theologian, Petrus van Mastricht. Cf. Mastricht, *Theoretico-practica theologia*, 12.

40. Sweeney, *Edwards the Exegete*, 197. Cf. *WJE* 22:80–102.

simply takes Romans in its canonical order and then inserts Edwards's comments on that section. This work represents a monumental task of locating and organizing Edwards's comments on any given text in Romans. For instance, in Rom 8:28 there are comments from the "Blank Bible," vol. 24; *A Treatise Concerning Religious Affections*, vol. 2; *Ethical Writings*, vol. 8; two entries from "Notes on Scripture," vol. 15; and two entries from the "Miscellanies," vol. 18.[41] The advantage to such research is that it collects Edwards's comments on any given text in Romans. However, it is not truly a commentary since it is not an exposition of Romans. The very nature of the project requires that Edwards's comments are uneven because they are included from a variety of contexts in Edwards's writings, not just explicit exegetical or expositional comments on Romans. It is also limited by its necessary neglect of dealing with Edwards's exegetical thought chronologically.

Also appearing in 2013 was the significant study of Stephen R. C. Nichols, *Jonathan Edwards's Bible: The Relationship of the Old and New Testaments*. Nichols focuses on Edwards's unfinished work, "The Harmony of the Old and New Testament." Edwards's "Harmony" was organized under three headings: prophecies of Messiah and their fulfillment, types of Christ and their antitype, and doctrine and precepts, or faith and practice. Nichols demonstrates that Edwards's work is in the context of certain Deists who were attacking the Bible, especially messianic prophecies.[42] Nichols argues that Edwards sought to "offer a defense of the unity of the Bible by arguing that a Messianic interpretation of the Hebrew Scriptures is a thoroughly reasonable and coherent interpretation of those Scriptures."[43]

Edwards was not writing a full-scale refutation of the Deists but was showing that such a christological understanding of the Old Testament was reasonable. Nichols also points out that Edwards took the Old Testament seriously in its historical context; he did not ignore the boundaries of the historical meaning for the sake of his own imaginative exegesis. Nevertheless, because Edwards believed in one ultimate author of the Scripture, to focus only on the intent of the human author would be inadequate to see the beautiful harmony of the Testaments. Edwards also believed that one not only needed to assiduously labor in the Word, but needed to have the assistance of the Holy Spirit: "Divine illumination is necessary for reading Scripture, but Scripture reading is no mystical experience detached from

---

41. Lovi and Westerhoff, *The Power of God*, 189–90.

42. Nichols, *Jonathan Edwards's Bible*, 56. "The storm created by Collin's *Grounds and Reasons* is the context of the first part of Edwards's harmony."

43. Nichols, *Jonathan Edwards's Bible*, 20.

exegetical rules."⁴⁴ Although Edwards was aware of the criticisms of the Bible, he offered only a reasonable alternative to the rationalistic approach of the Deists; the rationalists could not see what Edwards and the regenerate see because they lacked "new sense," that is the illumination of the Holy Spirit, which is necessary to see the divine intent.

Nichols argues that Edwards approach to the messianic prophecies are first "tightly constrained by Scripture."⁴⁵ Edwards's commitment to Scripture interpreting Scripture was unwavering. But so was his commitment to the necessity of the "new sense" which came by the Holy Spirit. Edwards's understanding of the Scripture, according to Nichols, was that the unifying theme was Messiah, his redemption, and his kingdom. Edwards noted, "Christ and his redemption are the great subject of the whole Bible.... The whole book, both Old Testament and New, is filled with the gospel."⁴⁶

Nichols shows that although Edwards was committed to a literal meaning of the text, the spiritual sense related to the literal meaning. When it came to the spiritual or divine authorial intention, Edwards was creative and innovative, although within his Reformed tradition. Nichols concludes his observation,

> In his approach divine authorial intention ultimately overwhelms that of the human author. Although Edwards believes that this divine intention may be communicated to one in possession of the Holy Spirit, the subjectivity of the whole exercise makes it all but impossible to reproduce to any practical effect. The rules that guide the saint in his or her reading of prophecy may perhaps be explicated. That they might be replicated is less certain.⁴⁷

The three major works, Nichols's *Jonathan Edwards's Bible*, Barshinger's *Jonathan Edwards and the Psalms*, and Sweeney's *Edwards the Exegete*, all highlight and explore Edwards's commitment to Scripture and his obsession with its interpretation. Although Sweeney's work is broader in scope than both Nichols's and Barshinger's, all three have overlapping but different emphases. Nichols emphasizes Edwards's focus on the dual authorship of Scripture, the human and the divine, and the subsequent necessity of the new birth to see the divine intent. Sweeney emphasizes Edwards's eclectic approach to Bible study, and the fact that Edwards did not have a uniform interpretive system when coming to biblical texts. Barshinger emphasizes

---

44. Nichols, *Jonathan Edwards's Bible*, 29.
45. Nichols, *Jonathan Edwards's Bible*, 56.
46. *WJE* 9:289–90.
47. Nichols, *Jonathan Edwards's Bible*, 56–57.

Edwards's redemptive-historical perspective, which largely encompasses his typological emphasis on Christ and the church.

Although Edwards as an exegete has certainly picked up momentum, there is still more work to be done on Edwards's treatments of specific books of the Bible. As Barshinger's work has shown, such an approach helps see Edwards in the environment of what he believed was his highest calling, a student, interpreter, and preacher of Holy Scripture. Such studies will help flesh out even more Edwards's own interpretive practices, his Bible-saturated world and life view, and him as a preacher of God's Word.

AN APOLOGIA FOR EDWARDS ON GENESIS

This survey of recent research on Edwards as an exegete has sought to demonstrate that there is much work to be done in different genres of Scripture. There have been various studies of Edwards's treatment of the Psalms, Proverbs, Isaiah, Jeremiah, Ezekiel, James, and Revelation.[48] One of the books of the Bible that stands out as neglected and yet vitally important is the book of Genesis. Genesis stands as a foundational book for the Bible, both for the origins and trajectories of redemptive-history and the great theological themes of God's work of creation, anthropology, hamartiology, covenant, and Christology. Genesis as history is apologetically important, especially considering critical evaluations of the book's historicity. Stephen Stein noted,

> Not only have devout believers often regarded the first five books of the Old Testament as foundational for their religious views, but these texts also have been a magnet for scholars preoccupied with the evolution of modern critical approaches to the Bible. Such critical studies were in the early stages of development during the years that Edwards was writing entries in the "Blank Bible."[49]

For these reasons, Genesis was profoundly important for Edwards. Edwards's own interest in redemptive history cannot be denied. Edwards was also actively engaged with those who wanted to deny the historicity of the Bible, especially Genesis. Edwards's theological interests consistently engaged the book of Genesis. Edwards's attention to Genesis is extraordinary.

---

48. Stein, "Like Apples of Gold," 324–37. Abernathy, "Jonathan Edwards," 815–30. Yoo, "Jonathan Edwards's Interpretation," 160–92. Stein, "Cotton Mather and Jonathan Edwards," 363–82. Kreider, *Jonathan Edwards's Interpretation*.

49. *WJEO* 24:24. Of course, this remains a contemporary concern as well, see Van-Doodewaard, *Quest for the Historical Adam*.

Edwards cites Genesis 1,940 times.[50] This is remarkable when one considers that the book of Psalms, which is three times the length of Genesis in terms of chapters, was cited by Edwards 4,204 times. Edwards cited Isaiah 3,852 times, the Gospel of John 2,203 times, and Revelation 1,183 times.[51] When one considers Edwards's strong affinities toward the Psalms, Isaiah, and John's writings, and then considers that Genesis is narrative, the number of citations is significant.

The use of Genesis in the corpus of Edwards's more than 1,200 sermons and writings, such as his "Blank Bible" (5,500 entries), "Notes on Scripture," *A History of the Work of Redemption*, and his "Typological Writings," needs further exploration because the book played a significant role in his theological thought, his biblical theology, and his public ministry.

Edwards used Genesis in a variety of ways. Quite noticeably, he used Genesis apologetically, especially in *The Freedom of the Will*.[52] Edwards uses Genesis twelve times in *The Freedom of the Will*, compared to thirteen uses of Romans. Edwards used numerous texts repeatedly as theological proof texts. Edwards certainly had his favorite Genesis texts as he expounded the Trinity, man's depravity, divine judgment, covenant, and sovereignty. Edwards also used Genesis extensively in his typological expositions. Edwards employs Genesis consistently as a foundational book for various *loci* of theology, and a rich field for typological exploration. Edwards preached twenty-two sermons from texts in Genesis.[53] In summary, while Edwards's attention to the first book of Moses is significant, the attention to the book of Genesis in Edwards studies has been lacking. Furthermore, Edwards's theology of the image of God, which is related to the first two chapters of Genesis, has also been lacking. This study attempts to address that deficiency.

PROPOSED METHOD OF STUDY

This study will employ the methods of historical theology. The subject matter is Jonathan Edwards's uses, comments, exegesis, exposition, and

---

50. A Scripture lookup on edwards.yale.edu, entering "Genesis," yielded 2,117 occurrences. The occurrences that were used by editors in the introductions or footnotes were deleted from the count. Where there were clear duplications or repetitions of the Scripture reference, as is common in "Notes on Scripture," only the first reference was counted. Occurrences which appeared in tables or lists of entries, for instance, like the one prepared by Benjamin Pierpont for the "Blank Bible" were also omitted. Edwards ends up citing the book of Genesis 1,940 times in his writings.

51. Barshinger, *Jonathan Edwards and the Psalms*, 7.

52. *WJE* 1.

53. *WJEO*, Sermon Index (Canonical).

theological appropriation of the book of Genesis. Edwards's commitment to the Bible as the supreme authority and divinely inspired is the foundation for Edwards's use of Genesis. Robert L. Calhoun has observed that the discipline of historical theology fits in with "neighboring disciplines in the curriculum."[54] This is certainly true in this case. How Edwards fit historically within the context of pre-critical and critical exegesis is a significant question, and sheds light on his exegetical approach. How Edwards fit historically with the Enlightenment and new criticisms against the Bible gives insight into the way that he often used the book of Genesis apologetically. Edwards as a pastor gives perspective on how he used Genesis in his preaching. Edwards's theological use of Genesis in the various *loci* of systematics reveals reliance on Genesis for much of his theological understanding. Each of these disciplines intersect in historical theology.

The method will be descriptive-analytical. The relevant sections of Edwards's massive corpus of written material will be examined in their historical context with a special emphasis on his use of Genesis. After describing Edwards's interpretive world, analysis will be given on where Edwards fit into that world. Furthermore, Edwards's resources and influences will also be explored. Any exegete and preacher of Scripture has influences in terms of books and people who help shape their understanding. As innovative as Edwards was, he did not come to Scripture in a vacuum, but rather he came to Scripture in a context where books were important, valuable, and relatively rare. Edwards came to Scripture within the Reformed and Puritan tradition but was not held in a traditional straitjacket. If there is a lack of attention on Edwards's use of Genesis, the main question for this study is how did Edwards make use of the biblical text of Genesis in his sermons and writings? A related question which emerges from Edwards's use of Genesis is, for example, what was Edwards's view of the *imago Dei*? This too is a neglected area that merits exploration, though not the main focus of this study.

Thus, although Edwards research is in full swing, in general, and Edwards as an interpreter of Scripture is also gaining momentum, more work needs to be done on Edwards's use of specific sections and genres of Scripture. There is no question about the foundational and even central role Genesis played in his thought and ministry. But does Edwards reveal a consistent interpretive approach as he deals with various sections of Genesis?[55] Certainly, Edwards used Genesis for a wide range of purposes, but as an interpreter, expositor, and preacher is there an observable, consistent method he used to interpret Genesis? What influences shaped his

---

54. Calhoun, "Role of Historical Theology," 444.
55. Namely, chs. 19, 3, 4, 32 (twice), 28, 12, and 39.

interpretive thinking? Although the focus of this study will be exclusively on Edwards, his sources and contemporaries will help identify where he belongs in the exegetical and theological tradition. Furthermore, how did Edwards specifically use Genesis to develop his anthropology (ch. 1 and then references to "image of God")? Part 1 of this study will be focused on Edwards's exegetical and homiletical use of Genesis in his sermons of the period from 1726–1735 (ch. 3) and 1736–1739 (ch. 4), with particular attention to the "Redemption Discourse" of 1739 (ch. 5). Part 2, emerging from part 1, serves an example of the theological relevance of studying Edwards's use of the book of Genesis. It will focus on Edwards's anthropology, with focus on the theology of the image of God (ch. 6). Although there have been many who have observed his theology on the nature of man, original sin, man's will, and affections, how did Edwards understand the image of God in his anthropology? Edwards on Genesis, then, may contribute further to the current portrait of Edwards as man wholly devoted to the Bible as an interpreter, theologian, and preacher.

Chapter Two

Edwards's Interpretive Tradition, the Enlightenment, and Critical Method

ROBERT BROWN, IN *JONATHAN Edwards and the Bible*, seeks to locate Edwards within the Enlightenment world of biblical criticism. Although Brown acknowledges that "Edwards clearly belongs to this stream of conservative interpretation,"[1] he then argues that

> though he did retain a high degree of confidence in the integrity of scriptural history, his approach was really a kind of hybrid traditionalism, one modified in significant ways by his accommodations to the new learning. He took seriously the implications and contributions that other disciplines (e.g., philology, history, epistemology, natural science) offered for understanding the biblical texts. In this sense, within the standards of the time, Edwards's approach is probably best described as "modestly critical."[2]

The observation that Edwards's approach is best described as "modestly critical," seems unhelpfully vague. Furthermore, to argue because Edwards used resources from other disciplines in his interpretive method that he was "modestly critical," ignores the fact that "precritical exegetes, in other

---

1. Brown, *Jonathan Edwards and the Bible*, xvii.
2. Brown, *Jonathan Edwards and the Bible*, xvii–xviii.

words, were not bereft of method merely because they followed a different method."[3] Stein's comments are too overly simplified to be helpful: "Pre-critical commentators carried out the interpretation of sacred texts within the confines of dogmatic or systematic theological commitments. Modern critics adopted an alternative set of exegetical procedures by turning to the philological, historical, and scientific study of ancient texts."[4] Sophisticated exegesis, relying on the latest learning, does not necessarily qualify as critical method. There is a difference between having a knowledge of critical methods and embracing those methods. Pre-critical exegetes employed the original languages, aids of history (for instance, Rabbinic studies), and more for their exegetical labors. Although Edwards would gather whatever knowledge he could to help him exegete the text, he remained within the stream of Reformed orthodox pre-critical exegesis, attested by his frequent use of Poole, Henry, and Doddridge.

The Reformed orthodox were commentators and exegetes *par excellence*. They applied their skills to the original texts of Scripture and produced commentaries and annotations of the Bible. Muller points out that they rejected the *quadriga* and utilized grammatical-historical insight from the original languages, biblical-theological readings of the text, consulting Jewish writings such as the Talmud, and often looking at the history of exegesis of the texts.[5] They poured themselves into scholarship, but not for the sake of scholarship. All the labor in the Word was for the sake of the church. No matter how profound the scholarship, the goal was to "instruct simple folk plainly in the knowledge of God."[6] This robust biblical scholarship was also the foundation of theology. "The Reformed orthodox, armed with a textually sophisticated but still technically 'pre-critical' method of biblical interpretation, were able to maintain and even to develop a churchly dogmatics throughout the seventeenth century."[7]

This was the Protestant and Reformed tradition to which Edwards very much belonged. Edwards adhered to the supreme authority of the Bible, the self-authenticating nature of the Scriptures, and the constant necessity to serve the church by interpreting and applying the Word. It is true, Edwards lived in the world of the Enlightenment, when pre-modern exegesis was giving way to critical methods. Enlightenment methodology

---

3. Muller and Thompson, "Significance of Precritical Exegesis," in *Biblical Interpretation*, 335.

4. Stein, editor's introduction to *WJE* 15:4.

5. Muller, *Post-Reformation Reformed Dogmatics*, 2:444–45.

6. Muller, *Post-Reformation Reformed Dogmatics*, 2:463.

7. Muller, *Post-Reformation Reformed Dogmatics*, 2:524.

rejected the methods and logical categories of medieval Aristotelianism and Scholasticism; in its metaphysics it tended towards naturalism or materialism; in faith it tended toward Deism. It believed in and acted upon the possibility of human progress, stressed the importance of the here and now as opposed to the hereafter, and had faith in the innate good of human beings.[8]

With the rejection of tradition and reliance upon autonomous human reason, biblical studies were revolutionized. Rationalist and critical exegesis rejected traditional and theological interpretation. The divine inspiration of the Bible was rejected, or at least sidelined as a working assumption. "The most primitive meaning of the text is its only valid meaning, and the historical-critical method is the only key which can unlock it."[9] The ideas of divine authorship, Scripture interpreting Scripture, and the necessity of the Holy Spirit were no longer the important components of interpretation. A transformed spiritual life was no longer the goal of biblical interpretation. "While higher-critical exegesis is engaged in careful research into philology and cognate studies, its goal is neither doctrine nor piety."[10]

It cannot be denied that Edwards was influenced by the seminal thinkers of the Enlightenment, such as Newton and Locke. Hall notes, "On the positive side, Edwards was a son of the Enlightenment, insofar as he took his intellectual cues from Newton and Locke. . . . On the negative side, however, Edwards had no truck with key Enlightenment trends like Deism, atheism, and free thought."[11] Nor is it denied that Edwards was a progressive thinker. Sweeney comments, "Edwards surely would have jumped at the chance to live with us today. He would have given almost anything for access to the historical and scientific knowledge that has burgeoned so dramatically since the early nineteenth century."[12]

Edwards was familiar with the world of biblical criticism. Edwards interacted with critical thought. Edwards was not opposed to new ideas, nor even being innovative in his own scholarship, nor was he averse to using the latest learning to serve his understanding of the text. However, Edwards's commitment to the divine inspiration of the Bible was unmovable. Edwards's firm conviction was that the Bible had dual authorship, God and the human author. Edwards notes, "God had a design and meaning which the penmen never thought of, which he makes appear these ways: by his

---

8. Hall, "Enlightenment," 198.
9. Steinmetz, "Superiority of Pre-Critical Exegesis," 28.
10. Neele, *Before Jonathan Edwards*, 8.
11. Hall, "Enlightenment," 199.
12. Sweeney, *Edwards the Exegete*, 4.

own interpretation, and by his directing the penmen to such a phrase and manner of speaking, that has a much more exact agreement and consonancy with the thing remotely pointed to, than with the thing meant by the penmen."[13]

Edwards was also insistent that in order to understand the divine author, one needed the new sense that comes in the new birth by the Holy Spirit. This work of the Spirit not only authenticates the Scriptures, but also enables one's ability to understand. Edwards preached that "there is a spiritual understanding of divine things, which all natural and unregenerate men are destitute of."[14] In that same sermon, Edwards would say, "There is an indisputable reason why none can teach the things of God but the Spirit of God: because none other can know the things of God but his Spirit. The Scripture is very full of this doctrine, that all spiritual saving light is given by the immediate teaching of God's Spirit."[15] The regenerate has new sight, new taste, new relish, and this spiritually equips the believer to hear God's words through the words of his penman.

Edwards's doctrine of Scripture was squarely in line with the pre-critical world of Reformed orthodoxy. Edwards's interpretive approach was exegetically robust, as well as fresh and creative. Edwards's goal in interpretation was not merely the acquisition of knowledge, but the acquisition of greater piety.[16] At every turn, Edwards was christological, theological, and practical in his relentless pursuit in the knowledge of God in the Bible.

EDWARDS'S EXEGETICAL RESOURCES

Jonathan Edwards, in his well-known sermon based on Hebrews 5:12, "The Importance and Advantage of a Thorough Knowledge of Divine Truth," exhorted his congregation, "Procure, and diligently use other books which may help you to grow in this knowledge. There are many excellent books extant, which might greatly forward you in this knowledge, and afford you a very profitable and pleasant entertainment in your leisure hours."[17] Edwards took his own advice and diligently used books to help him understand the Scriptures.

13. *WJE* 13:347–48.
14. *WJE* 14:72.
15. *WJE* 14:89.
16. "Seek not to grow in knowledge chiefly for the sake of applause, and to enable you to dispute with others; but seek it for the benefit of your souls, and in order to practice." *WJE* 22:102.
17. *WJE* 22:101.

Edwards's Interpretive Tradition, the Enlightenment, and Critical Method 21

Edwards's world of books has fascinated Edwards's scholars for decades. "Edwards's world was therefore a culture of the book to its core."[18] Stephen J. Stein notes that Edwards possessed his own personal library, and he borrowed books from friends, fellow ministers, his father, Timothy Dwight, and from the library of the Hampshire Association of Ministers.[19]

Edwards learned Latin and Greek from his father, Timothy Edwards. Edwards's Yale education was composed of learning logic, rhetoric, science, mathematics, Latin, Greek, and Hebrew. In his library Edwards had a well-used copy of Johann Buxtorf's *Manuale Hebraicum et Chaldaicum*. Buxtorf (1564–1629) was a Reformed Protestant Hebraist.[20] The flyleaf indicates this was a gift from Edwards's father. Another Hebrew language resource was gifted to him from David Brainerd, *Lexcion Hebraicum et Chaldaicum*, which was another volume from Buxtorf. Edwards referred to this volume frequently. Edwards also had in his possession the Antwerp Polyglot. As for Edwards's language skills, his Latin and probably his Greek would have been excellent. However, his Hebrew was probably weaker, although he worked hard with the tools he had.[21] Edwards, ever wanting to learn and improve his own knowledge and ability, upon taking the presidency of Princeton, expressed his desire to improve his Hebrew by teaching it to the students.[22]

Edwards had three favorite commentators: Matthew Poole, Matthew Henry, and Philip Doddridge. Matthew Poole (1624–1679) had produced his monumental work, *Synopsis Criticorum aliorumque Sacre Scripturae*, from 1669–1676. Neele observes,

> In summary, the *Synopsis* is a composition of a vast number and variety of authors of various faith traditions, though mediated and appropriated into the framework of the *Synopsis*; a delta of philological and etymological exposition of the texts of Scripture in the service of biblical exegesis—an observation that cannot be neglected when examining Edwards's use of Poole's *magnum opus*.[23]

In Edwards's "Blank Bible" he cites Poole 792 times. However, it is significant to observe that the majority of those citations are found in his comments on the Pentateuch (211 times), the historical books (299 times),

---

18. Theusen, editor's introduction to *WJE*, 26:2.
19. Stein, "Edwards's Sources," 24:59.
20. Sweeney, *Edwards the Exegete*, 14.
21. Sweeney, *Edwards the Exegete*, 16.
22. Sweeney, *Edwards the Exegete*, 17.
23. Neele, "Early Modern Biblical Commentary and Jonathan Edwards," in Barshinger and Sweeney, *Jonathan Edwards and Scripture*, 56.

and wisdom literature (263 times).[24] It appears that Edwards leaned more heavily on Poole for the Old Testament and Doddridge's *Family Expositor* for the New Testament. Neele notes, "Edwards's use of the *Synopsis*, then, was not an exception—though the degree to which he used it surpassed that of many before and after him."[25]

In Edwards's "Blank Bible," he cites 109 sources. Some of these Edwards owned, some he borrowed. But it is clear that Edwards saw the value of availing himself to whatever resources helped him to better understand the text. Edwards was no ordinary preacher studying his Bible for a sermon. Sweeney notes, "Edwards devoted most of his waking life to studying the Bible, its extra-biblical contexts, its theological meanings, and its import for everyday religion. His student and friend, Samuel Hopkins, once remarked of his priorities: 'He studied the Bible more than all other Books, and more than most other Divines do.'"[26]

---

24. *WJE* 24:60.

25. Neele, "Early Modern Biblical Commentary and Jonathan Edwards," in Barshinger and Sweeney, *Jonathan Edwards and Scripture*, 59.

26. Sweeney, *Edwards the Exegete*, 5.

PART ONE

Exegetical and Homiletical

Chapter Three

Jonathan Edwards's Exegesis of Genesis

Genesis Sermons (1727–1735)

"Although the reputation of Jonathan Edwards is appropriately multi-faceted . . . the popular conception of him as a preacher is essentially correct."[1] Before the analysis of Edwards's sermons on Genesis, something should be said about Edwards as a preacher and how he approached the task. Preaching was in the air that Edwards breathed. "As son of the village parson, the young Edwards was reared in the ecclesiastical-academic atmosphere of a home where sermons were always in the making,"[2] notes Wilson Kimnach. The influences on Edwards's preaching would have been his father, Timothy Edwards and his maternal grandfather, Solomon Stoddard. "Timothy Edwards was a powerful and successful preacher, by all accounts."[3] Solomon Stoddard, however, was one of the "great preachers of the latter days of the Massachusetts theocracy."[4] Both men would have a lasting impact on Edwards as a preacher.

The literary influences on Edwards as a preacher are seen in his own catalogue of books. Edwards would have read John Edwards, *The Preacher* (London, 1705), and Cotton Mather's *Manuductio ad Ministerium* (Boston,

1. *WJE* 10:3.
2. *WJE* 10:4.
3. *WJE* 10:11.
4. *WJE* 10:12.

1726).⁵ The most popular handbook on preaching was John Wilkins's *Ecclesiastes*, which was methodologically Ramist. Wilkins taught that the sermon was to be divided into three parts: explication, confirmation, and application. This threefold division was common in Puritan preaching.

Additionally, with Edwards's known fondness of Peter van Mastricht (1630–1706), he would have been familiar with Mastricht's 1681 disputation included in *Theoretica-Practica Theologica*, called "the Best Method of Preaching." Furthermore, the influence of William Perkins's *The Arte of Prophesying*, was still in full force in Edwards's New England. Kimnach notes, "But it would not have been necessary for him to study the art of 'prophesying' abstractly, for the tradition of New England pulpit oratory was very much alive in Edwards's day; moreover, it was embodied in the very person of Timothy Edwards."⁶ Edwards inherited a sermonic form which was shaped by the Puritans and consistently practiced by his examples.

Edwards employed the tripartite division of the sermon consistently throughout his ministry. Edwards would begin with the text of Scripture, often accompanied with a brief explanation of the text. This opening of the text would include various observations about the text. From the text, Edwards would then draw out the doctrine, typically in the form a simple proposition or thematic statement. The doctrine would then be supported or expanded by proofs or observations. "The proofs of the doctrine are of two basic types: citations of Scripture (often attended with interpretation), and appeals to human reason and commonplace experience."⁷ The final section of the sermon was the application, called "improvement" or "uses." This is the part of the sermon that is applied directly to the hearers. Application is made to unbelievers, believers, young, and old. The application was the most powerful part of the sermon since it was specifically addressed to the minds, affections, and consciences of the hearers. Variations to this structure can be seen over the course of Edwards's ministry, but as Kimnach observes, "it is evident that Edwards never lost sight of the paradigm."⁸

GENESIS SERMONS (1725–1735)

Of the known extant sermons, Edwards preached from Genesis twenty-two times. This does not include occasions when Edwards would have repreached a sermon elsewhere. The analysis of these sermons will be chronological,

5. *WJE* 10:16.
6. *WJE* 10:10.
7. *WJE* 10:38.
8. *WJE* 10:37.

which entails a problem or two. First, Edwards did not start dating his sermons until 1733. There are also undated sermons from 1734–1739 and 1743–1758. There are only three printed Genesis sermons published in the Yale edition.[9] Six of the twenty-two sermons are transcripts.[10]

Edwards's first sermon from Genesis is "Warnings of Future Punishment Don't Seem Real to the Wicked."[11] The sermon was preached in late 1727, when Edwards was about twenty-four or twenty-five years old. It was August of the previous year that Edwards was invited to assist his grandfather, Solomon Stoddard, at Northampton. In February 1727, Edwards was ordained as assistant pastor. This makes this the fourth sermon that he preached at Northampton.[12] The sermon text is Gen 19:14, "And Lot went out, and spake unto his sons-in-law, which married his daughters, and said, Up, get you out of this place; for the Lord will destroy this city. But he seemed as one that mocked to his sons-in-law."[13]

Solomon Stoddard had taught that a sign of bad preaching was "when men don't preach much about the danger of damnation."[14] George Marsden observes that for Stoddard,

> the Duty of preachers was clear. They must warn people that they trod on the brink of eternal misery. To fail to do so was to lack human feeling. . . . Stoddard must have been pleased to hear Edwards's early sermon in Northampton on *The Warnings of Future Punishment Don't Seem Real to the Wicked.*[15]

Edwards employs Lot's warnings to his sons-in-law as the basis of his sermon. Edwards interprets Lot positively, as a righteous man, in light of 2 Pet 2:7–8, but ineffectual in his preaching to the wicked. In his overview of the context he makes one exegetical note, that the word "mocked" is used in Judg 16:10. "'And Delilah said unto Samson, Behold, thou hast mocked me and told [me

---

9. *WJE* 14:198–212; 17:329–48; 19:418–34.

10. Sermon nos. 199, 200, 381, 434, 464, 504. The remaining thirteen are known but either have no surviving manuscripts or not been transcribed yet. The printed sermons and transcripts will be analyzed. The other sermons from Genesis are as follows: Gen 6:22 (Sept. 1740); Gen 27:39 (Apr. 1741); Gen 43:3 (Feb. 1742); Gen 15:1 (July 1742); Gen 24:58 (July 1742); Gen 19:17 (July–Dec. 1741); Gen 25:29–34 (ca. 1741–1742); Gen 4:3–5 (Nov. 1743); Gen 12:3 (Nov. 28, 1744); Gen 3:4 (Dec. 1746); Gen 1:27 (Aug. 1751, Stockbridge); Gen 32:24–32 (May 1754, Stockbridge); Gen 3:17–19 (Apr.–Dec. 1756).

11. *WJE* 14:198–212.

12. Schafer and Neele, "Chronological List," 10.

13. Edwards repreached this sermon, as numerous editorial endnotes reveal.

14. Quoted in Marsden, *Jonathan Edwards: A Life*, 119.

15. Marsden, *Jonathan Edwards: A Life*, 120.

28   Part One: Exegetical and Homiletical

lies]'; that is, 'You cheated me and pretended to tell me where your great strength lay, to make a fool of me.'"[16] Edwards does not make a direct correlation however, between Delilah's words and the words of the sons-in-law, only to say that they did not give heed to Lot's warning. Edwards then draws out the doctrine from the text, "The reason why men no more regard warnings of future punishment, is because it doesn't seem real to them."[17]

Edwards unfolds the doctrine and explains why it is that some do not believe in future punishment and have no apprehension of it.

> Now the greater part of men have not a lively sensible apprehension of the wrath of God and of eternal punishment; it never was set before their eyes and brought into clear view. They have very little of a notion what the wrath of God is, and so it doesn't appear very terrible to them. They have but a faint dull idea of the misery of the damned: and that is the reason that, when they are told of it, it doesn't terrify them.[18]

Edwards then explains why men do not regard the warnings of future punishment. "Sin has a great influence to benumb and stupefy the understanding, and to make plain and certain things seem like uncertain dreams and fables."[19] In the application, or the improvement of the doctrine, Edwards seeks to do two distinct things. First, he seeks to convince men how unreasonable and absurd it is to deny future punishment. Second, he attempts to drive home a "lively sensible apprehension of this punishment."[20] Edwards distinguishes between knowing something theoretically and apprehending it with the senses, to feel it. In this second use, Edwards vividly describes what happens to the soul when it is taken to hell. As Edwards concludes the sermon, his appeal is very limited, only exhorting his auditors not to disregard the threats and consider the brevity and uncertainty of life.

In this early sermon, Edwards expounds the text as history, but then uses Lot's sons-in-law as types or examples of refusing to heed a warning of future punishment. There is not much gospel in the sermon, it is predominantly warning. It appeals to the reason and to the senses, with sound arguments and vivid imagery. The theme of judgment, well taught by Edwards's father and grandfather, would hold a significant place in his preaching, as demonstrated at this early stage. That Edwards's thoughts were much on

16. *WJE* 14:201.
17. *WJE* 14:201.
18. *WJE* 14:202.
19. *WJE* 14:206.
20. *WJE* 14:209.

eternal punishment at this time is attested to as Edwards writes in his "Miscellanies" about hell or torment in hell multiple times.[21]

Edwards next sermon from Genesis was entitled "East of Eden," preached from Gen 3:24, "So he drove out the man; and he placed at the east of the garden of Eden cherubim, and a flaming sword which turned every way, to keep the way of the tree of life."[22] This sermon was preached July 1731.[23] Stoddard had died February 11, 1729. Edwards became the senior pastor. "With Stoddard's death, and having exhausted his stock of previously written sermons, he increased his pace of sermon composition markedly. Yet Edwards's private affairs were basically stable. He remained for the most part in Northampton, growing accustomed to the steady rhythms of pastoral life."[24]

Edwards's treatment of Gen 3:24 may have been a lecture. There was typically a Sunday morning sermon, a Sunday afternoon sermon, and then a Thursday lecture. Mark Valeri notes, "The length of a typical two-preaching-unit sermon (eighteen leaves), it has no indication that Edwards did divide the sermon into preaching units—a further indication, beyond the lengthy Doctrine, that this was a lecture."[25] There are several features to this sermon which stand out, besides its length.[26] First, it is profoundly theological. The sermon is rich with doctrinal content pertaining to the covenant of works, the covenant of grace, original sin, total depravity, Christ's active and passive obedience, and Christ as the second Adam who restores paradise, but superlatively so. The other feature that stands out is Edwards's use of language. The vividness of this sermon is consistently remarkable. Whether Edwards is describing Adam's agonizing loss or Christ's glorious restoration, Edwards's language is visual and affectional. Finally, the sermon focuses much more on the gospel and Christ than the previous Genesis sermon, preached three and a half years prior.

The time frame for the sermon is around the time Edwards preached the Boston Lecture, which was later published as *God Glorified in the Work of Redemption*. Edwards was focusing on the doctrine of sin and man's inability due to the fall, perhaps seeking to undermine Arminian influences or tendencies in Northampton. "Edwards anticipates arguments that he would later use

---

21. Minkema, "Chronology," 4. See Miscellanies 279, 280, 282, 288, 316, 318.
22. *WJE* 17:329–48.
23. Neele and Schafer, "Chronological List," 29.
24. *WJE* 17:4–5.
25. *WJE* 17:330.
26. *East of Eden* is nearly 8,500 words, while Edwards's previous Gen 19:14 sermon was approximately 5,400 words.

in *Original Sin*."[27] Valeri claims that "*East of Eden* incorporated a political critique in a discussion of Adam's fall." Although Edwards was actively engaged in the politics of his day, and spoke on political or civic topics, there is nothing in this sermon which indicates "a political critique," unless of course one assumes that Edwards's view of original sin and total depravity were subtle critiques of the political landscape. Rather, Edwards as theologian and pastor is emphasizing the misery of the fall and the glory of Christ's redemption.

Edwards opens the sermon on Gen 3:24 with these words: "This chapter is the most sorrowful and melancholy chapter that we have in the whole Bible."[28] Edwards spends considerable time developing the context of Genesis 3. Edwards makes two observations, the first is that Genesis 3 gives us an account of "our first parents' loss of their former blessedness," and second, an account of the "irrecoverable loss (that is, irrecoverable by them) of eternal life and those blessings, by their fall, which otherwise they would have obtained."[29] Edwards then deduces two doctrines. "I. When man fell, God drove him away from all his former blessedness. II. When we fell, we so procured the displeasure of God that there was no hope by anything that we could do of ever attaining that life and eternal blessedness which otherwise we should [have] attained."[30] It should be noted that two doctrines are deduced; the first deals with Adam, the second with humanity: "When man fell. . . . When we fell."

Edwards unfolds the doctrine through several propositions. It is in these propositions that some of Edwards's vivid and warm expressions shine. For example, "Man enjoyed the favor of God and smiles of heaven; there were smiles without any frowns. He had communion with God; God was wont to come to him and converse as a friend and father. How sweet was it thus to have the smiles and fellowship of the glorious Creator!"[31] Edwards expounds on the fall of Adam and graphically describes his loss, creating a sense of melancholy. In the second doctrine he explains why human beings can no longer obey God. "There was no hope of our ever obtaining for ourselves this eternal life and blessedness after we had fallen. When we fell we not only were driven away from all that blessedness that we did enjoy, but lost all that which we had so fair an opportunity of obtaining."[32]

---

27. *WJE* 17:329.
28. *WJE* 17:331.
29. *WJE* 17:332.
30. *WJE* 17:332.
31. *WJE* 17:334.
32. *WJE* 17:339.

God's anger and displeasure against sin is the next topic. Edwards is focused as the sermon develops; he does not stray off topic. There is a force to the logical progression of the sermon. "The anger of God for the apostasy of man was not the anger of a father but of an enemy. God before was as a father to man and loved him as a child. He had communion with him as a friend. But now God became man's enemy."[33] Edwards persuasively demonstrates God's just wrath against fallen humanity who "cast contempt upon God's majesty." The sword of divine wrath, just like the flaming sword in the Garden, is wielded by an offended God. Edwards concludes his supporting propositions, "These two doctrines may give us something of an idea of the melancholy and doleful loss that man sustained by the fall."[34]

Edwards then does something which he did not do in his first Genesis sermon, he quickly moves to the gospel. Edwards speaks in rapturous terms of the glad tidings proclaimed to Adam's fallen children. In a moving application, Edwards speaks of God's grace bringing back his enemies through his Son.

> After we have despoiled ourselves of all our primitive excellency and loveliness and become odious and in the image of Satan, we may have God's beauty put on us again; yea, we may be brought to perfect holiness as spotless as that which we lost. God is willing to restore our whole man, to exalt our faculties to a like strength and vigor with that which we had before, and our bodies to the like beauty and life. This corruptible may put on incorruption and this mortal immortality.
>
> 'Tis proclaimed in the gospel that God is willing again to receive us into his favor, to pardon all our sins, to quit all enmity, to bury all former difference and to be our friend and our father; that he is willing again to admit us to sweet communion with him, and that he will converse with us as friendly and intimately as he did before the fall; and that God is willing to receive us to paradise again, to a like freedom from all grief and trouble; that he will wipe away all tears from our eyes, and that sorrow and sighing shall flee away; that he will make us to forget our former melancholic, forsaken, and doleful state; that we may be again admitted to as great a fullness of blessings, to as pleasant and delightful a dwelling place as the garden of Eden, as full of those things which tend the delight of life, to pleasures as refreshing and satisfying; and we shall be as free from want. The curse shall be removed, and all frowns and tokens of displeasure. The world

33. *WJE* 17:340.
34. *WJE* 17:342.

shall again smile upon us and congratulate us. God will be our friend and the angels shall be our friends, and all things shall be at peace with us, and we shall enjoy as great and uninterrupted a pleasure in mutual society.

The wrath of God drove us out of paradise, but the grace of God invites us to return. The Son of God in the name of his Father comes and calls to us to return from our banishment; he ceases not to call us. He beseeches us to return again. He is come forth on purpose to make known those joyful tidings to us. Christ calls us away from this cursed ground, that brings forth briars and thorns, to a better country. Our first parents were driven away very loath and unwilling to go, but we are invited back again.[35]

Edwards preaches Christ in the application with power and beauty. Christ reversed Adam's fall. Christ restored what Adam lost. Christ succeeded where Adam failed. Christ by his death opens up the tree of life. Indeed, Christ is the tree of life. "Christ's obedience is a more glorious obedience than Adam's would have been and rewarded with a better reward."[36] It is God's wisdom that accomplished this great reversal. Edwards preaches Christ as the substitutionary wrath-bearer, who takes the flaming sword for those driven out by it. "Christ himself was slain by that flaming [sword]; and this sword, having slain the Son of God appearing in our name, who was a person of infinite worthiness, that sword did full execution in that."[37] Edwards addresses the fact that man in his natural state has no ability to see that sinners are saved by the righteousness of another. He points out that they think they are good enough. Edwards concludes with a warning to those who "have a high opinion of their own worthiness, excellency, good deeds, prayer, [and] religion, [but are] ignorant what a distance [is] between God and them,"[38] and an appeal to seek the tree of life.

This lecture-sermon brings together Edwards's historical view of the fall, the theological implications of the fall, and then a christological focus which draws out the typology of Adam and Christ and the tree of life. Edwards's skill in using descriptive, vivid, and emotive language is clearly developing. There is a weaving together of history, theology, typology, and Christ-centered application, all expressed through gripping, emotive language.

35. *WJE* 17:342–43.
36. *WJE* 17:344.
37. *WJE* 17:346.
38. *WJE* 17:348.

Edwards next two sermons in Genesis were preached sometime between August 1731 and December 1732, apparently back-to-back. The first of the two is numbered as sermon "199. Gen 4:7. 'Wicked men's sins lie at their door.'"[39] It is a transcription of Edwards's notes.[40] The second of the two is numbered as sermon "200. Gen 32:26–29. 'The way to obtain the blessing of God, is not to let God go except he bless us.'"[41] This sermon is also a transcription of Edwards's notes.[42] This sermon, however, was published as *The Blessing of God: Previously Unpublished Sermons of Jonathan Edwards*.[43]

Edwards's preaching environment was not only one of coming judgment but one of revival. Both his father and grandfather had seen periods of revival. "Zeal for evangelism was the cutting edge of their campaign."[44] Thus, preaching for the awakening of sinners was part and parcel of preaching. The sermon Edwards preached from Gen 4:7 was an evangelistic sermon. The text, "and if you dost not well sin lieth at the door," is an exposition of God's words to Cain after God had expressed approval of Abel's offering and disapproval of Cain's.

In the explanation of the text, Edwards follows Matthew Henry's view on why Abel's offering was acceptable, and Cain's was not. Edwards states, "It was not the fruits of the ground that Cain offered were not good in themselves that God did not accept them, but it was because the heart that offered them was not good. Abel offered his offering with faith, Cain not. Heb. 11:4, by faith Abel offered a more excellent sacrifice than Cain."[45] Matthew Henry stated, "The great difference was this, that Abel offered in faith, and Cain did not."[46]

The doctrine that Edwards extracts is this: "That wicked men's sins lie at their door." The implications of this doctrine are: "The sins that they have committed, all of them, as to the guilt of them, still remains."[47] Edwards goes on at some length to point out that even though the acts of sins committed are soon over, and there is nothing visible remaining, the wicked moves on

---

39. Schafer and Neele, "Chronological List," 30.
40. *The Works of Jonathan Edwards Online* (hereafter *WJEO*), 46:199.
41. Schafer and Neele, "Chronological List," 30.
42. *WJEO* 46:200.
43. Edwards, *Blessing of God*, 13–28.
44. Marsden, *Jonathan Edwards: A Life*, 116. "Their campaign" refers to William Williams's and Solomon Stoddard's vision for the "prosperity of their people under God's covenant" (116). The campaign revolved around (1) a strong clergy, (2) preserving Reformed orthodoxy, and (3) zeal for evangelism.
45. *WJEO* 46:199.
46. Henry, *Exposition*, 1:38. See also, Poole's *Synopsis, in loc. WJE* 24:141.
47. *WJEO* 46:199.

as if these sins are done. But they are not done, something does remain, their guilt remains. The guilt for every single sin remains. Time does not lessen the guilt; it remains in full force against them. "Though they seem to them to be but little sins, yet as they were sins the guilt abides and they can't remove it, they can't abolish it, do what they will, there they will be."[48] The wicked may forget their sins, but God never does; he maintains his book of accounts.

The second implication is that the guilt of their sin stands at the ready to bring the wrath and judgment of God upon them, "as an enemy lay waiting at a man's door to destroy him."[49] Because God does not forget, wrath and judgment hangs over the wicked, as one would lie in an ambush, or as an enemy would wait at the door to kill at the first opportunity. "They are waiting for opportunity; they are waiting for God's time to destroy them. They hunt for the precious life."[50] Edwards's imagery evokes a fearful picture. The sins of the wicked, which they have forgotten about, have already kindled the fires of hell, and eternal death is watching and waiting. Edwards does something unusual; he illustrates this with a rather lengthy story, "I have read of a one in South America that . . ." Edwards tells a story then of a man who provoked and resolved to kill the man who had affronted him. The one trying to avoid his enemy travelled 960 miles over fifteen days, and 1,200 miles over twenty days. Yet the avenger did not give up the pursuit until he had killed the man in his own house, on his own bed. Edwards then says, "so much more closely does men's guilt follow and their sins pursue them wherever they go. Men's sins still lie at their door."[51]

The application of the sermon is wholly evangelistic. The first use is to awaken sinners. Edwards urges his listeners to "consider this that their sins lie at their door as mortal enemies watching for their destruction."[52] Edwards appeals to his listeners not to make light of their sins, but to consider what their sins deserve, indeed, that the curse and wrath of almighty God is at their door. Edwards exhorts them to consider the sins of childhood, the sins of youth, sinful thoughts, how they had sinned with their tongues and their hands. "There will be no such thing as fleeing when God's time comes. You will be then like a man that is encompassed all around by enemies with

---

48. *WJEO* 46:199.
49. *WJEO* 46:199.
50. *WJEO* 46:199.
51. *WJEO* 46:199.
52. *WJEO* 46:199.

mortal weapons and there will be no escaping. You shall be met with whatever way you endeavor to make your escape."[53]

The second application is: "Your sins that lie at your door are there waiting for the appointed time of your death—that is the time for them to do their execution."[54] Just like an enemy waits to kill, so sin is simply waiting for death for their opportunity to seize the sinner. The third application: "Consider that you are never safe one moment as long as sin lies at the door. Destruction is waiting for you and you know not when it will come upon you."[55] To live with sin at the door is to live in constant danger. After Edwards expounds these three applications, he gives a "use of exhortation," which is, "Give yourself no rest till you have obtained that your sins should be removed from your door."[56] The only way to live in peace and safety is to have those sins removed and the only way they can be removed is through Jesus Christ and his blood. Christ's blood is sufficient to take away their sins, take away their guilt, and remove these enemies from the door.

This sermon is directed completely to the unconverted. It is wholly evangelistic. There is ample exposition of the context of Genesis 4 within its historical context. Edwards uses Cain typologically, as a negative example of a careless sinner. The sermon does not delve into great theological themes, it goes after the conscience. The sermon concludes by pointing the listeners to Jesus Christ and the wonderful experience of sins forgiven.

The next sermon in Genesis, presumably preached right after the Gen 4:7 is from Gen 32:26–29, "And he said, Let me go, for the day breaketh. And he said, I will not let thee go, except thou bless me. And he said unto him, What is thy name? And he said, Jacob. And he said, Thy name shall be called no more Jacob, but Israel: for as a prince hast thou power with God and with men, and hast prevailed. And Jacob asked him, and said, Tell me, I pray thee, thy name. And he said, Wherefore is it that thou dost ask after my name? And he blessed him there." The sermon's title: "The way to obtain the blessing of God, is not to let God go except he bless us."[57] Edwards would preach this text again in 1735 and then at Stockbridge in 1754. Mark Noll comments, "Edwards was occupied with this text early, late, and in the middle of his career."[58] The purpose of the sermon is to encourage persistent

---

53. *WJEO* 46:199.
54. *WJEO* 46:199.
55. *WJEO* 46:199.
56. *WJEO* 46:199.
57. Schafer and Neele, "Chronological List," 30.
58. Noll, "Jonathan Edwards's Use of the Bible," 33.

prayer. Although "the blessing" is undefined, Edwards exhorts his congregation to pray with affection and earnestness.

Edwards opens the context for this 1731–32 sermon by reviewing the circumstances of Jacob preparing to meet an angry Esau. Edwards interprets Jacob staying in the rear quite positively, namely that he would have a better opportunity to "pour out his supplications to God and seek his favor and mercy at this juncture."[59] Edwards then identifies the man who wrestled with Jacob as the Second Person of the Trinity, the Son of God. The Son of God "had undertaken to be man's Mediator and Surety and was to take on him the human nature was wont frequently under the Old Testament to appear in human shape, probably sometimes occasionally assumed a human body before his proper incarnation."[60]

After this christological interpretation of the man who wrestled Jacob, Edwards then gives a speculative reconstruction on how the wrestling began. "I will venture to inform you what appears to me to be the probable."[61] Edwards reconstructs the scene by positing that the man came to Jacob that night and began conversing with him. The conversation was clearly with an "excellent and amiable person." The visitor was speaking to Jacob in a "condescending and friendly manner." Jacob was thoroughly delighted with his visitor and their conversation. Then the stranger acted as if he was going to leave. Jacob was unwilling to let the visitor go, he wanted "to have more of his company." The man strives to leave, but Jacob holds him back, "hence followed a wrestling between them."[62] The doctrine that Edwards drew from this was, "The way to obtain the blessing of God is to resolve not to let God go, except he bless us."[63]

In Edwards's explanation of the doctrine, he begins by telling his auditors what it does not mean by "not letting God go except he bless us."[64] This "not letting go" is not demanding from God based on debt. "Pay me what thou owest . . . thy blessing is my due I have merited it."[65] Nor is it seeking the blessing without doing the proper deeds, such as the use of proper

---

59. *WJEO* 46:200. Both Matthew Henry and Matthew Poole interpret Jacob staying in the rear positively, for the purpose of prayer. "He desired to be in private, and was left alone, that he might again more fully spread his cares and fear before God" (Henry, *Exposition*, 1:195). "In some private place, it matters not on which side Jabbok, that he might more freely and ardently pour out his soul unto God" (Poole, *Annotations*, 1:75).

60. *WJEO* 46:200.

61. *WJEO* 46:200.

62. *WJEO* 46:200.

63. *WJEO* 46:200.

64. *WJEO* 46:200.

65. *WJEO* 46:200.

means or turning from lusts. Nor is it "persevering in seeking a blessing in a remiss and unresolved manner."[66] Edwards says that believers cannot seek the blessing in an inconsistent or unsteady way, or for just a limited time. Finally, it is not asking it of God and at the same time expecting it from ourselves. Edwards thoroughly lays out the arguments of what seeking the blessing is not.

Edwards then expounds the way of seeking the blessing, and he begins by pointing his listeners to the way Christ taught his disciples to seek the blessing in prayer. Edwards marshals texts from Luke 18 and the importunate widow; Luke 11:5 and the parable of the man who went to his neighbor's house at midnight; and the Canaanite woman in Matt 15:21. Edwards says there is great encouragement in these texts. Edwards moves to reasons why God has ordained this manner of obtaining the blessing. This way, says Edwards, those seeking show their sense of need and value of it. Delay in receiving the blessing causes the seeker to reflect on their own unworthiness of the blessing. Furthermore, it causes the seeker to acknowledge God as the author of the blessing. Finally, such earnestness in wrestling prepares one for the blessing.

Edwards concludes the sermon with the application. In a brief evangelistic appeal, Edwards points out that the greatest blessing is being converted. Edwards then applies the sermon to two sorts of persons. "First to those who have for a long time been doing something for a blessing and have had no success."[67] Here Edwards points out that perhaps the earnestness has been short-lived, or the world is hindering the "the success of your seeking a blessing . . . when you have received awakening impressions by the word or providences, have not the cares of the world soon wore them off and crowded out the thought of them?"[68]

Edwards makes an evangelistic application to the older ones in the congregation. "Do you find that there arise more difficulties in this affair of seeking your salvation as you grow older don't you find that your heart grows harder."[69] Edwards's relationship with the elderly in his congregation would grow increasingly strained. "Edwards, though an adherent of a hierarchical world view, espoused a developmental theory and a view of the will and habit that emphasized the formative period of youth, and a system of

---

66. *WJEO* 46:200.
67. *WJEO* 46:200.
68. *WJEO* 46:200.
69. *WJEO* 46:200.

signs of grace that indicted the aged for their unbelief."[70] At this early stage, Edwards is warning the elderly against hard-heartedness.

The second sort of person Edwards addresses is those who "are but newly setting out in seeking a blessing if any such are here present."[71] Edwards gives three warnings that they may be in danger of. The first being that they would look at themselves as being more in earnest than they really are. The second is self-flattery and then discouragement. The third danger is having "carelessness steal upon you insensibly." This danger erodes conviction by degree.

Edwards would preach this passage and sermon again in August 1735. It seems unusual that Edwards would preach the same sermon within a four-year period. However, the Connecticut Valley revivals began in December 1734. Throughout 1735 Edwards was preaching awakening sermons.[72] The sermon published as "Blessed Struggle" is reemployed in the revival context to encourage earnest perseverance in seeking the blessing, just like Jacob did when he wrestled with the angel of God. Edwards uses much of the same material from the 1731–32 sermon, sometimes even the same phrasing. Edwards certainly understood this event in Jacob's life as historical, and he expounds it as such. But he also sees Jacob as a type of the believer in prayer. "We have here, and in the context, a remarkable account of Jacob's wrestling with God, as he appears to him in the form of a man; by which we are to understand a literal wrestling, as striving to overcome in that bodily exercise, thought typical of something spiritual."[73]

Edwards will repeat that the wrestling was literal, but he will draw out facets of the event as a typological pattern for prayer. "Jacob's thus wrestling with God, was doubtless ordered in providence, and recorded in Scripture history, to be a type and representation of prayer; of that fervent, and earnest, and persevering prayer, in which we ought to seek the blessing of God."[74]

Edwards makes four observations about Jacob's trial and perseverance. God opposed Jacob, so there was a struggle; the longer the trial continued, the more it looked like God was opposing Jacob; God put Jacob's thigh out of joint, but Jacob was resolved, just like the Canaanite woman of Matt 15; Jacob would not let go of God, even though God told him to. The doctrine is, "It is frequently God's manner, when persons are seeking the blessing

---

70. Minkema, "Old Age and Religion," 703.

71. WJEO 46:200.

72. Schafer and Neele, "Chronological List," 47–50.

73. WJE 19:422.

74. WJE 19:424. Matthew Henry had made the same observation. "It was not only a corporal, but a spiritual wrestling, by the vigorous actings of faith and holy desire; and thus all the spiritual seed of Jacob, that pray in praying, still wrestle with God" (1:195).

of him, to exercise them with trials of their resolution and steadfastness in seeking, before he bestows it upon them."[75] The first time Edwards preached this text, his doctrine was simpler: "The way to obtain the blessing of God is to resolve not to let God go, except he bless us."[76] In this preaching, Edwards focuses on the trials God puts in the way of the person seeking the blessing as a test of their resolution.

Edwards goes at this theme from a variety of ways, reminding his congregation, "Such a way of seeking is most agreeable to the value and importance of the thing sought; to seek such a good with thorough earnestness, resolution, and perseverance, is but treating it suitable to its nature."[77] Although the blessing is somewhat ambiguous at this point in the sermon, Edwards says it is incredibly valuable and worthy of such effort. Edwards then outlines, almost tediously, how many ways God can make obtaining the blessing difficult. But the more difficult, the more earnestness, and the more earnestness, the more prepared one is to prize the mercy and glorify God for it.

As in the first preaching of this sermon, Edwards employs the Canaanite woman (Matt 15:22–23) and blind Bartimaeus (Mark 10:46–48) as examples of those who were apparently opposed but did not give up. Throughout the sermon, Edwards uses phrases like, "Thus it was Jacob," "So it was with Jacob," "as Jacob." Edwards is underscoring that Jacob is the pattern for the one seeking the blessing. Sometimes, Edwards points out, it gets darker and darker the longer one seeks, but this is only a test of one's steadfastness. In the end, it is a reminder to the seeker that they do not get the blessing in their own strength.[78] The trials and the humiliation of seeking without obtaining shows the seeker what he is, how he ought to despair of himself, and how dependent they are on God's mercy.

In the application Edwards has a specific target in mind, those who have not yet been converted in the revival. Maybe they have been seeking the blessing of salvation, but then been discouraged. "Hence what cause have they to lament that [they] have failed, and been discouraged under trials they have met with, in their seeking, because God hid his face from them?"[79] The trials were only designed to see "whether you would be steadfast [in

---

75. *WJE* 19:425.
76. *WJEO* 46:200.
77. *WJE* 19:436.
78. "It was not in his own strength that he wrestled, not by his own strength that he prevailed, but in and by the strength derived from heaven" (Henry, *Exposition*, 1:196).
79. *WJE* 19:434.

seeking]. [It was] no sign at that [God] never [intended his blessing]."[80] Edwards charges those who became discouraged with backsliding, which is grievous in light of the "remarkable pouring out of God's Spirit that has been among us."[81] Edwards then urges those who are seeking salvation not to give up, but to persevere. He deals with certain objections but exhorts them to press on.

Throughout this sermon Edwards is conscientiously committed to the historical or literal meaning of the text, but his typological uses of multiple facets of the event dominates his preaching of the text. Edwards sees the text christologically, but the focus centers on the typological patterns for his listeners to follow. The context of revival gives Edwards an urgency in pressing Jacob's steadfast perseverance in the face of obstacles on those who have yet to obtain the blessing of salvation.

Edwards seemed to have an incredible fondness for this passage. Edwards cites this text together with the Canaanite woman in correspondence in "Apocalyptic Writings."[82] Edwards uses the text in his "The Life of David Brainerd" to illustrate Brainerd's prayer life: "But it must be observed that when he set about this duty, he did it in good earnest; 'stirring up himself to take hold of God' and 'continuing instant in prayer' with much of the spirit of Jacob, who said to the angel, 'I will not let thee go, except thou bless me.'"[83] Edwards mentions the text twice in "A History of the Work of Redemption," once in "Typological Writings," and three times in "Notes on Scripture." The fact that he would preach the same sermon twice, within approximately four-year period reveals something of his fondness for it.

Edwards's earliest sermon from Genesis was among his first preached at Northampton. Edwards developed quickly as a preacher. The preaching in this early era was deeply theological, as evidenced by "East of Eden." Edwards preaching also exhibited evangelistic emphases, as in the sermon on Cain from Gen 4:7. Perhaps most significantly was Edwards wider use of typology, especially in establishing exemplary patterns for believers to follow, as in the two sermons on Jacob from Genesis 32. Edwards's exegesis of the text was shaped both by pastoral concerns and application, as well as explorations in the typologies of Scripture.

In summary, these sermons from the book of Genesis in the period 1727–1735 show Edwards's careful attention to the text. Not only are there clear hints of exegesis underlying the sermon, but the context of the passage

---

80. *WJE* 19:434.
81. *WJE* 19:434.
82. *WJE* 8:446.
83. *WJE* 7:531.

is always set forth. The doctrine is also derived directly from the text. Edwards's carefully crafted doctrine statements where then supported and applied. Edwards also demonstrated early on his ability to draw out theology from the text. Edwards's exegesis was often theological exegesis, expounding the great truths of the Reformed faith. Edwards also showed a developing skill in typology, as well as exemplary preaching. For Edwards, typological and exemplary coalesced when he used OT figures as a type of believer or unbeliever, and then made pointed moral and evangelistic applications to his audience.

Chapter Four

Jonathan Edwards's Exegesis of Genesis

Genesis Sermons (1736–1739)

THE PERIOD CA. 1735–1737 of Edwards's Northampton pastorate has been identified as the Connecticut Valley revival and precedes the so-called Great Awakening of the early 1740s. Edwards would preach another Genesis passage on Jacob in March 1736, Sermon 381, Gen 28:12, on Jacob's ladder. The sermon is a transcript.[1] The previous year had been a challenging one for Edwards, although it was a time of awakening, "Satan seemed to be more let loose, and rage in a dreadful manner."[2] There was an attempted suicide in March of 1735. Then, Joseph Hawley Sr., Edwards's uncle, committed suicide by cutting his own throat.[3] There was an ordination controversy over Arminianism and health issues that fall. By the end of the year, the church had voted to build a new meetinghouse. Edwards's sermons in the new year, 1736, were pastoral and evangelistic. In February 1736, Mrs. Esther Warham Mather Stoddard died. Edwards preached her funeral sermon from Rev 14:13b, "When the saints depart out of this into another world, their works do follow them."[4] Edwards followed Mrs. Stoddard's funeral sermon with a sermon on Jacob's ladder.

1. *WJEO* 51:381.
2. Quoted in Marsden, *Jonathan Edwards: A Life*, 163.
3. Marsden, *Jonathan Edwards: A Life*, 163.
4. Schafer and Neele, "Chronological List," 51; sermon 380.

GENESIS SERMONS (1736–1739)

The text is "and he dreamed and beheld a ladder set upon the earth and the top of it reached to Heaven," Gen 28:12. This sermon is incredibly long, extending to over nine thousand words in the transcript. There is an indication that it may have been preached in two sermon units. At almost the midpoint, approximately 4,100 words into the transcript, the text and doctrine are repeated, "Gen 28. 12. doc. The ladder which God hath set on the earth for men to ascend to happiness reaches even onto Heaven."[5] It appears that this is where Edwards started his second sermon unit on the text. This sermon, like the others, is both historical and typological. However, Edwards's typological interpretation of this text extends in many different directions. Whereas his typology in the previous sermons had been christological and exemplary, in this sermon Edwards goes to a different level.[6]

Edwards briefly gives the context of Genesis 28, and then says, "The vision that he had of the ladder is doubtless typical of spiritual as indeed all divine visions are representative of spiritual things."[7] Edwards then states that the typology in this passage represents two things; the first is Jacob as a type of Christ. Edwards appeals to Isa 49:3 where the Messiah is called Jacob. Then he appeals to John 1:51 where the angels are ascending and descending on the Son of Man. So Jacob represents Christ. But Edwards pushes the type even farther. Jacob's sleep in Genesis 28 is typical of the death of Christ. Christ by his death opened the gates of heaven, just as Jacob in his sleep saw the gates of heaven opened. The ladder is nothing other than the covenant of grace itself, procured by Christ's death.

Edwards then takes the typology in another direction; Jacob also represents the believer or the church or spiritual Israel. Then Edwards pushes the type even farther again. The stone that Jacob laid his head upon "represents Christ who is from time to time compared to a stone and is the Rock or stone on which believers rest."[8] The stone was anointed; Christ is the anointed one. The stone at Bethel represents the temple or house of God. Christ says of his own body that it is the temple of God. Furthermore, the stone upon which Jacob rested was used to set up a pillar and as an altar. "Therefore, there can be no dispute but that Christ the Great Altar on which all our spiritual offerings much be offered was typified by it."[9] Edwards

---

5. *WJEO* 51:381.

6. Edwards's extensive typological treatment of this text is outlined in his "Blank Bible," *WJE* 24:172–76.

7. *WJEO* 51:381.

8. *WJEO* 51:381.

9. *WJEO* 51:381.

pushes the type even more. The stone is also a type of faith, by which the believer rests on Christ. "Jacob while resting on this stone has Heaven's gate opened to him and a ladder reaching from him to God in Heaven so it is by faith in Christ whereby believers rest on Christ that they have Heaven's gate opened to them."[10]

All of these typological observations are a part of his explanation of the text. It is only after extensively exploring these types that Edwards gets to the doctrine. A full one-quarter of the first sermon is devoted to a detailed typological interpretation of Jacob's dream. The doctrine is "the ladder which God has set on the earth for man to ascend to happiness reaches even unto Heaven."[11] Edwards expounds the doctrine under four major headings. The first is the simple observation that God has set a ladder on the earth for men to ascend to happiness. The second is an explanation of what the ladder is. The third is to show that it reaches to heaven. The fourth is that it provides for ascending to such a height.

Edwards points out that fallen mankind needs a ladder to climb out of the sin and misery of this world. The ladder indicates man's need of deliverance from destruction. The ladder "is the way and method of salvation that God has provided in Jesus Christ. It is by Christ alone there comes to be such a ladder set down on the earth for poor sinful man to ascend on out of a state of misery to a state of blessedness."[12] Edwards then brings back into focus his earlier typological observations. The ladder is a type of Christ, a type of the covenant of grace; believers, like Jacob need to rest on Christ; there is no other way of salvation than resting on Christ. This ladder of salvation brings miserable man into a state of happiness and enjoyment of God. "But this ladder reaches far above all such changes to a world of immutable and eternal glory and blessedness."[13] This final statement appears to end the first sermon.

The second sermon begins with the third heading, "How God provides and makes a way for our ascending to such a height."[14] Edwards immediately answers by stating that heaven belongs to Christ, and Christ in the covenant of redemption unites believers to himself, so since he is the possessor of heaven and earth, the believer's union with Christ secures heaven for him. Edwards then explores the death of Christ as that which makes a way for believers to ascend to the heights of heaven. Christ made complete atonement

10. *WJEO* 51:381.
11. *WJEO* 51:381.
12. *WJEO* 51:381.
13. *WJEO* 51:381.
14. *WJEO* 51:381.

for sin and removed the obstacle between heaven and earth. Christ paid the price for the believer to enjoy heaven. In the resurrection Christ has gone into heaven and there "remains as a public person as the head of believers. He has gone as the first fruits."[15] The believer is united to Christ by faith, so heaven is his. Finally, Edwards points out that Christ will return to take believers, both in body and soul, to heaven.

The application focuses on self-examination. Edwards asks his listeners to inquire whether they are ascending toward heaven. A person cannot try to climb up on their own, that is vain. Such a climbing will only meet God's wrath. It is Christ alone who is the only way. Edwards in the application revisits again that the stone of Bethel was a type of Christ and so urges his listeners to look to him in trust and hope. "Jacob rested and had sweet repose on the stone of Bethel. So has your soul rest and acquiescence to the way of sovereign grace revealed in the Gospel."[16]

Edwards is emphatic that Jacob's ladder is not ascending on one's own righteousness. There are certainly men, who in their imagination, seek to climb by their own righteousness, but that claim results in falling deeper into hell. Edwards spends some time in developing the idea that not to be on the ladder is to be in this world which will be destroyed with the fire of God's judgment. Sinners must get on the ladder of the covenant of grace, and when they do, the angels who ascended and descended on Jacob's ladder will minister to them (Heb 1:14). Few find this ladder, which Edwards equates with the narrow gate (Matt 7:14).

Edwards concludes with application to the Christian. The Christian's life is spent climbing this ladder, fighting against the weight of the body and the flesh and the inclinations toward the corruptions below. The Christian must strive in his upward climb to the fountain of blessedness. Such a promise of the future should keep the Christian stirred to continue to ascend. The glory of God and the paradise of God and eternal rest will be theirs who labor to climb.

These two sermons stand out from the others preached from Genesis so far in Edwards's career. First, Edwards stays true to form in dealing with the text historically and typologically, but in these sermons, the typological is extensive. Edwards is far more specific in tracing out the typological significance of details in the text. Second, the sermon is very evangelistic. Edwards preached faith in Christ clearly. On multiple occasions he exhorted to listeners to rest in Christ alone as the only method of ascending into

15. *WJEO* 51:381.
16. *WJEO* 51:381.

heaven. Edwards emphasized union with Christ and only by virtue of that union does the believer possess heaven.

The next sermon Edwards preached from Genesis was in June 1737. It was repreached in September of 1753.[17] This sermon is based on Gen 12:2, "And I will of thee a great nation and I will bless thee and make thy name great and thou shalt be a blessing." The setting of the sermon is early June 1737, by which time there was already a noticeable spiritual decline after the revival two years before. This may have caused some embarrassment for Edwards since *A Faithful Narrative* was not even available in the colonies yet. In the *Faithful Narrative*, Edwards proclaimed that nearly everyone in town was showing hopeful signs of grace.[18] However, old rivalries and divisions had reemerged.

On March 13 of that year, the meetinghouse gallery had collapsed. What most certainly should have resulted in serious injuries and death turned out to be "one of the most amazing instances of divine preservation, that perhaps was ever known in the land."[19] Despite such a preserving providence, a contentious spirit continued in the town, one which had plagued Northampton for many years. Edwards preached a sermon published as "Underserved Mercy," from Ezek 20:21–22. The original title was "When God's professing people behave themselves unanswerably to great things that God has done for them, God sometimes appears ready in [an] awful manner to destroy them, and yet in undeserved and wonderful mercy withdraws his hand and spares them. . . . For a day of prayer appointed on occasion of the front gallery's falling, which fell on Mar. 13, 1737."[20] Instead of repentance and seeking God's blessing, the contentions continued. A new meetinghouse was built, and again there was strife. "The town's seating committee had to rank each family in relation to every other."[21] The ranking was determined by wealth, then public service, and finally age. Patricia Tracy notes, "Age had always taken precedence over wealth, but a majority of Northampton's voters implied that property was more respectable than old age, that worldly achievement was more laudable than experience as a humble Christian—and this was only two years after the revival of 1735!"[22]

---

17. This would have been during Edwards's time in Stockbridge and was probably delivered to the English congregation. The symbol *(D)* at the top of the transcript indicates that Edwards intended to use some of the content of this discourse in his "The History of Redemption" project.

18. Marsden, *Jonathan Edwards: A Life*, 184.

19. Quoted in Marsden, *Jonathan Edwards: A Life*, 184.

20. Schafer and Neele, "Chronological List," 58.

21. Marsden, *Jonathan Edwards: A Life*, 186.

22. Tracy, *Jonathan Edwards, Pastor*, 126.

It is in this context that Edwards preached Gen 12:2. The sermon is quite long, running over ten thousand words. It was probably delivered over two preaching occasions. Whereas the previous Genesis sermon, preached less than a year before, was filled with typology, this sermon is almost exclusively a hortatory type of message, without much theological depth or typological interpretation. One can detect that Edwards's pastoral concerns for the attitudes and strife present in the congregation. Edwards opens Genesis 12 with the historical background of the call of Abraham. Edwards utilizes Heb 11:8 to show that Abraham answered the call by faith, which led to his obedience. Edwards then points out that there are two observable parts. The first is "that God would bless Abraham."[23] "The other part of the promise is that God would make him a blessing."[24] Unlike the sermon on Jacob wrestling with the angel, there is minimal use of Abraham as a type or example for the believer. Edwards notes, "He is made a blessing to the Church of God in all ages of the world by this eminent example of his faith and obedience that is transmitted down for the use of all."[25] The doctrine is "what is greatly to be desired is to be blessed of God and to made blessings unto others."[26] Edwards then unpacks both points in the doctrine. The first great blessing from God that every person should desire is spiritual life, freedom from bondage, blindness, and death, and God putting them out of the reach of hell.

The blessing of God results in happiness. Edwards spends considerable time developing the idea that being blessed by God is both safety and happiness, and that happiness is unshakable, even if "all the men in world and all the devils in hell should join together to hinder it."[27] There is a beauty and sweetness to the blessing of God, it changes people. This leads Edwards into the second proposition, "That it is greatly to be desired that [we] should be blessings to others."[28] Edwards says that persons can be a blessing to others outwardly, "by contributing to others prosperity, their wealth and outward state."[29] This would have peculiar relevance to the congregation as those were wealthier had just been recognized for their wealth by the seating committee.

The best way to be a blessing, says Edwards, is "by being made the means and instruments of good to other souls. Some men are made great blessings in this respect that they are the instruments not only of outward

23. *WJEO* 52:434.
24. *WJEO* 52:434.
25. *WJEO* 52:434.
26. *WJEO* 52:434.
27. *WJEO* 52:434.
28. *WJEO* 52:434.
29. *WJEO* 52:434.

good and of their salvation from hell and being happy forever."[30] This is the most excellent blessing to others. But Edwards points out there are other ways to bless others. Reproving sin, recovering them from their backsliding, instructing them, and promoting religion are all ways to bless one's neighbor. Edwards then delineates why it is desirable to be a blessing to others. First, he states that it is an "excellent and lovely thing to do good to others."[31] There is a duty to do what God has commanded; it reflects being a child of God (Matt 5:45). Edwards then contrasts the loveliness of "dispersing benefit to all around" with the very "unlovely sight to see a man that is all for himself and not for anybody else."[32]

Edwards tells his congregation that God puts great honor on those who bless others. It is an honor to be a benefactor to others. Furthermore, it is not only an honor, it brings peace and comfort to mind. Doing good to others brings true pleasure, since it is "more blessed to give than to receive" (Acts 20:35). The pleasure of doing good to others is far greater than the pleasure of "getting and scraping together and hoarding up for themselves."[33] Edwards then takes his listeners to their deathbed, "How uncomfortable and dreadful must it especially be on a death bed to look back on a past life and to have it to consider that he has done little or no good in his life that he has lived in vain and been a mere cumber [i.e., a hindrance or burden] to the earth."[34] The next motivation to being a blessing to others is that those who bless others are esteemed and loved. They have a good reputation with others (Prov 22:1). They also have a reward in heaven. The day of judgment will bear out the good that they have done to others.

Edwards then brings both themes back together, in what may be the beginning of the second preaching occasion. "Proposition: It is very desirable that those two things should go together that they that are blessed of God themselves should be made blessings to others."[35] Edwards then expounds on how gratitude to God should obligate the Christian to do good to others. When the Christian considers the blessing which God has bestowed on him by giving his only Son and the blessings that his blood has procured, they should strive to be a blessing. To experience God's blessing and favor should make the Christian pity the destitute and seek to bless them.

30. *WJEO* 52:434.
31. *WJEO* 52:434.
32. *WJEO* 52:434.
33. *WJEO* 52:434.
34. *WJEO* 52:434. The language perhaps reflects Edwards's disappointment with the elderly, whom he perceived as hindering the awakening.
35. *WJEO* 52:434.

If we are truly thankful for Christ's being at great cost to purchase a blessing for us then we have a sense of that excellency of his kindness in being at such cost. And if we are indeed sensible that it is an excellent thing to be at cost and suffering to help others then we shall not be backward to it ourselves.[36]

The application of the sermon immediately focuses on the threat of the curse and judgment of God. A person who is under the curse of God is a curse to others. The pastoral context of the sermon makes this application especially pointed toward those who refused to help others in time of need, or who sought personal advantage at the expense of others. "If God curses a man none can help. He is miserable and will be miserable if he remains under God's curse. All the world can't keep him from being miserable and undone."[37] Rather, a person should greatly desire to be blessed by God and be a blessing to his people. This is the way of true happiness.

Edwards's next use in the application section is a call for self-examination. Edwards says to his congregation that if they think they have received blessing from God, they need to ask whether they have been a blessing to others. To be blessed to be a child of God is the best blessing of all, but such a blessing changes the heart toward others. "Those who have truly blessed themselves with the saving grace of God's Spirit are of a spirit to pity others under their calamities."[38] Edwards then brings up the spiritual decline in the Northampton Church. "It has been some considerable time since a great number here present have entertained that hope that they were blessed of God. How have you lived since? Have you been as selfish as you used to be before and as little concerned for the good of others and negligent of it?"[39]

The application section extends beyond the typical length. Edwards doggedly continues, asking question of heart motives and actions. Is their light shining? Do they appear to be children of God? Do they imitate their heavenly Father? "Herein you will excellently answer the end of your creation, who are not made for yourself only, but for others. Also consider how that in this way only you can well fill up your place in human society."[40] Edwards relentlessly returns to compelling his hearers to consider God's blessing on them and to consider the example of the Lord Jesus Christ and what a blessing he was to others. Edwards then says, "I would mention two things further in particular besides those things that were suggested in the

36. *WJEO* 52:434.
37. *WJEO* 52:434.
38. *WJEO* 52:434.
39. *WJEO* 52:434.
40. *WJEO* 52:434.

doctrinal part, as motives to influence you to labor that you may be a blessing to others."[41] Edwards tells his congregation to make sure when they are blessed by God to be sure to increase that blessing by diffusing and communicating it to others. This, says Edwards, is the best way to grow and improve the grace that is given. Edwards also states that blessing others now is the best way to bless one's children and lay up "portions for posterity."

Edwards continues the application by laying out all the various relations where the congregation could be a blessing: families, husbands and wives, parents, in town, places of public trust, ordinary secular callings. Edwards exhorts them to labor to be a blessing on every occasion and take every opportunity. They are even to bless enemies. Edwards is not yet finished. He gives directions in closing. Saints who are truly holy are a blessing. If saints are not a blessing to others it is because of weak grace. They need to labor after a spirit of meekness and love. They should not expect much good to be done to them if they are not doing good to others. Edwards closes with these words: "If therefore you would be a blessing in the world, be content to live a life of self-denial."[42]

This sermon demonstrates that Edwards was not just a theologian in the pulpit, or a creative typologist and exegete. Edwards went into the pulpit with deep pastoral concerns. In this sermon Edwards takes the twofold statement to Abraham, that God would bless him, and he would be a blessing, and applies it to his congregation relentlessly. The sermon is an exhortation, and a tedious one at that. The sermon is an assault on the spiritual apathy that had set in, as well as an assault on the party-spirit, arrogance, and selfishness that had often marked the town and the church. The transcript reflects a pastor who is belaboring the application, often repeating the same points, in order to make sure he is heard.

Edwards next sermon in Genesis was less than a year later in March 1738. Edwards preached Gen 39:12, "And he left his garment in her hand and fled and got him out."[43] "It is a duty not only to avoid those things that are themselves sinful, but also, as far as may be, those things that lead and expose to sin."[44] The sermon was repreached in March 1757 and published as "Joseph's Great Temptation and Glorious Deliverance."[45] The discourse

---

41. WJEO 52:434.
42. WJEO 52:434.
43. WJEO 53:464,
44. Schafer and Neele, "Chronological List," 62.
45. WJEO: Sermon Index (Canonical), #464. Genesis 39:12. Published in Hopkins, Life and Character, 2:24–58.

was delivered over two sermon units.⁴⁶ The transcript is rough, with many lined out words and sentences, as well as choppier sentences than the other transcripts.⁴⁷

The sermon uses Joseph's escape from temptation in a typological and exemplary manner. Joseph is a type of believer facing temptation. However, like the Gen 12:2 and unlike the Genesis 32 sermons, the typological emphasis is somewhat minimal. Edwards's emphasis is almost entirely exemplary with an ethical focus. The application reveals Edwards's pastoral concerns, especially for the young people in the congregation. Edwards was deeply concerned about the conduct of the young people, going back as far as 1729. By March 1738 Edwards once again took up the sins of the young people. "Edwards continued his periodic attacks on the sexual sins of young people and the heinous indulgence of their parents."⁴⁸ The sins Edwards was mainly concerned about were bundling and carousing. Bundling was "the New England practice . . . in which parents allowed young people to spend the night in bed together partly clothed."⁴⁹ "Bundling, which was supposed to be a way of getting acquainted without sexual intercourse, did not always work as advertised. Pregnancies before marriage were rising dramatically in New England, even in well-churched Northampton."⁵⁰ Carousing consisted of staying up late into the night "frolicking," which led to other vices. "Edwards was fighting not only youthful sexuality but also parental permissiveness."⁵¹

Edwards opens the text in his normal way, by expounding the background to the text. Edwards unfolds the context of Genesis 39 with detail, making numerous observations. Edwards observes first how great the temptation was that Joseph was under. "It is to be considered that Joseph was now in his youth, a season of life when persons are most liable to be overcome by temptations of this nature."⁵² Edwards spends considerable time exploring this first observation by delving into the greatness of Joseph's temptation. Edwards details Joseph's escape and then concludes that Joseph's fleeing temptation and Potiphar's wife's way of temptation "is doubtless recorded

---

46. The date reads, "March 5 7 ( ) March 1738." *WJEO* 53:464.

47. Also, Edwards uses an "x" in Scripture references, so "Gen x 39 x 12 x" and in abbreviations, for instance, "afterwx."

48. Tracy, *Jonathan Edwards*, 130.

49. Marsden, *Jonathan Edwards: A Life*, 130.

50. Marsden, *Jonathan Edwards: A Life*, 131.

51. Tracy, *Jonathan Edwards*, 131.

52. *WJEO* 53:464.

for our instruction."[53] Edwards then draws out the doctrine: "It is our duty not only to avoid those things that are themselves sinful, but also as far as may be those things that lead and expose to sin."[54] Edwards urges his congregation to avoid those things which could lead to temptation, then he compiles his arguments.

The arguments revolve around sin as a great evil which brings great harm. Sin is the greatest evil and it should be plain that Christians are required to earnestly avoid it. "Sin is an infinite evil because against an infinitely great and excellent being and so a violation of infinite obligation."[55] Edwards also argues that Christians should avoid sin because they have a sense of its evil and should have a just hatred of it. Edwards also appeals to general observation that men avoid things that hurt or ruin them temporally. If a man avoids that which brings temporary ruin to temporary interests, how much more ought he to avoid those things which bring eternal ruin. Edwards labors through these arguments, warning of the danger and the harm that come from sin and so should be avoided at all costs.

Edwards then reminds his listeners that when they pray the Lord's Prayer, they are praying that they would not be led into temptation; "certainly we ought not to run ourselves into temptation."[56] Edwards compiles biblical admonitions from Jesus and Paul, warning his congregation to be watchful and even ruthless against sins. "Yea, Christ tells us that we must avoid them however dear they are to us though they are as dear as our right hands or right eyes."[57] Edwards warns of idolatry, and his congregation's own sense of weakness. "He who trusts in his own heart is a fool" (Prov 28:26). With these arguments the first preaching unit comes to an end.

The second preaching unit begins with the application. "To exhort all to a compliance with their duty in this respect, not only to avoid sin, but those things that lead to and expose to sin. If it be made out clearly and evidently from reason and the word of God to be our duty so to do, this one would be enough with all Christians."[58] Edwards anticipates those who might object by asking, "How shall we know what things do lead and expose to sin."[59] Edwards answers that this is much clearer than some would suggest, and it cannot be denied without "the greatest absurdity." First, men's

---

53. *WJEO* 53:464.
54. *WJEO* 53:464.
55. *WJEO* 53:464.
56. *WJEO* 53:464.
57. *WJEO* 53:464.
58. *WJEO* 53:464.
59. *WJEO* 53:464.

hearts incline them to certain lusts, and knowing that they should avoid anything that borders on them. If the Israelites built parapets to keep people from falling off their roofs and being killed (Deut 22:8), then Christians should recognize that lusts are strong enemies, drawing a man into sin, and he should stay as far away from the edge as possible.

Edwards goes on to point out that those things which feed the lusts in the imagination are of this same sort and should be avoided. Edwards utilizes Matt 5:27–28 to warn of the imagination that can feed lusts. He warns, "we are command to keep at the greatest distance from spiritual pollutions and to hate even the very garment spotted with the flesh Jude 23."[60] Edwards then appeals to a person's experience and personal observation and what their natural tendencies are. Men learn much by experience, such as sun and rain showers bring forth plants, and certain kinds of serpents bring illness and even death. So men should learn from the natural tendencies of their own hearts, "Thus we may determine that tavern haunting and gaming are things that tend to sin because common experience and observation shows that those practices are commonly attended with a great deal of sin or wickedness."[61]

Edwards then makes an argument from the outpourings of God's Spirit, saying that they may determine that a thing be evil by the effect that an outpouring of God's Spirit had on it. When religion is flourishing, a pouring out of God's Spirit may put a stop to certain customs and practices, which is a sure sign that it is evil. Another means by telling the evil of a practice is to consider if it was openly and universally practiced, instead of done in secret or partly hidden. The reaction would be enough to indict certain practices. In these arguments, or rules, as Edwards would call them, he is really going after those who may have been trying to justify certain practices.

Edwards next target is the young people. "And particularly I would now take occasion to warn our young people as they would approve themselves servants of God, to avoid all such things in company that being tried by those rules will appear to have a tendency as lead to sin."[62] Edwards attacks the young people's customs of the country at large. Then Edwards takes up the practice of bundling, "that custom in a particular manner of young people of different sexes lying in beds together; however light is made of it and however ready persons may be to laugh at its being condemned; if it be examined by the rule that have been mentioned it will appear past

60. *WJEO* 53:464.
61. *WJEO* 53:464.
62. *WJEO* 53:464.

all contradiction."[63] Edwards denounces the practice as that which stirs up lusts and leads to gratifying those lusts. Then he addresses those who think they are in no danger when they engage in the practice. They think they can easily overcome temptation, but Edwards reminds them of Peter's false self-confidence. The warning is against getting comfortable with the temptation and "by venturing further and further they fell at last into the foulest and grossest transgressions."[64] In an interesting description of the temptation, Edwards says that some young persons, with respect to the sexual sin, are dealt with by the devil like someone charming a bird or a serpent, being under the spell.

Edwards addressed the sins of late-night gatherings, spending the night "for mirth and jollity that they all frolic and so spending the time together till late in the night."[65] Edwards then pleads with the young people to listen to him since what he says, he says as a messenger of the Lord of hosts. A true Christian will listen to such a message because a true Christian is willing to have his practices examined and tried by the rules of God's Word. Indeed, the true Christian rejoices in having ways tried. Here Edwards gives a homiletical preemptive strike against those who would question his wisdom or authority. Edwards then criticizes the country in sweeping indictments against young people. Throughout the country the young people are irreligious, vain, loose, and "those persons that are the greatest frolicked and are most addicted to this practice of we are speaking, they are the people farthest from being serious."[66] Edwards appeals to the young people, asking them to examine themselves and see if such practices have not indisposed them to serious religion. Edwards reminds the young people that they have a great advantage, "because there has lately been here in this very place a most remarkable pouring out of the Spirit of God. The most remarkable that ever has been in New England and it may be in the world since the apostles' day."[67] Edwards's next strategy is to point out that the return to such customs may be hindering the work of the Spirit among in the present time.

Edwards deals with objections to his application. The first objection is interesting. The interlocutor says in effect the current circumstances of the town are not the same as they were, and although there was a concern then to put an end to these practices, there is not the same concern now since it is not seen as harmful. Edwards's answer is easily anticipated. If such a

---

63. *WJEO* 53:464.
64. *WJEO* 53:464.
65. *WJEO* 53:464.
66. *WJEO* 53:464.
67. *WJEO* 53:464.

practice was a hindrance to true religion then, it is certainly a hindrance now. The rule which was true then is still true. Edwards strongly condemns the practices not only as tending to sin, "but is in itself very disorderly, sensual, shameful, for it is attended late in the night, in the dead of the night to the neglect of family prayer and violating all family order, which is disorder and profaneness."[68]

The next objection is that the wise man in Ecclesiastes says there is a time to mourn and a time to dance. Edwards is quick to point out that the dancing approved of in Scripture was not the frolicking kind of dancing being practiced. The wise man also says there is a time to kill, but no one thinks they need to go out and murder. Edwards answers yet another objection: if all the ways of the young people are amended, they will be ignorant how to conduct themselves in mixed company. "If we go abroad, we shall be ashamed to be appear dull and awkward and appear as mere mopes [i.e., pessimists, killjoys]."[69] Edwards ridicules this objection, stating that the objection claims, "The pouring out of the Spirit of God upon a people tends to make mere mopes or gumps [i.e., dolts] of them."[70] The reality is that such an outpouring makes holy persons, heirs of eternal life, and so such an objection is to "talk so blasphemously of it."[71]

In the conclusion, Edwards urges his listeners that those who are converted, especially among the young people, will find the arguments and rules satisfying. Edwards calls on heads of families not to tolerate such practices among their children. The final exhortation is for the serious consideration of these things "of all persons old and young."[72]

Edwards's treatment of Genesis in this discourse is almost exclusively exemplary for ethical purposes. Even Edwards's references to Joseph are minimal. At many points in the sermon, he could have alluded to Joseph again, but the pastoral concern and application is consumed not so much with the typology of Joseph, as it is with the pastoral casuistry, driven by his concerns for his young people. This sermon, like the Gen 12:2 sermon, shows that Edwards the exegete is also Edwards the pastoral preacher, who preaches occasional sermons, influenced and shaped by pastoral concern.

In February 1739 Edwards preached four sermons from Gen 3:11, "Hast thou Eaten of the tree whereof I commanded thee that thou shouldest

---

68. *WJEO* 53:464.
69. *WJEO* 53:464.
70. *WJEO* 53:464.
71. *WJEO* 53:464.
72. *WJEO* 53:464.

not eat."⁷³ This is the second discourse Edwards preached from Genesis 3. It is critical to observe that Edwards would begin his monumental "A History of the Work of Redemption" in March 1739. An analysis of Edwards's use of Genesis in that will work will be provided in the next section; however, it is important to note that for Edwards, *A History of the Work of Redemption* would be a major undertaking. It appears that Edwards's four-unit sermon on Gen 3:11 as well as some of his other studies were in preparation for his larger project.

Edwards will refer to Genesis 3 seventeen times in *A History of the Work of Redemption*. More than half of those references deal with the fall; the rest use Gen 3:15 as the first gospel promise. In Miscellany 788, "Imputation of Adam's Sin. How," Edwards references his own sermon, "God had respect not only to Adam but his posterity. See my third sermon from *Genesis 3:11*, the first use. And also [proved] from the nature of all covenant transactions in Scripture."⁷⁴ Miscellanies 717, 785, and 786 also deal with the fall, the covenant of works, and the imputation of Adam's sin. Miscellany 717 references his third sermon from Gen 3:11. It appears that not only was Edwards occupied with this theme in 1739, but that it was a theme that fascinated him for nearly the next twenty years of his life.

The discourse on Gen 3:11 is delivered in four parts and draws frequently on the imagery and themes covered in *East of Eden*.⁷⁵ The first sermon unit unfolds Adam's delightful communion with God in the Garden and then expounds God's interrogation of Adam after he ate from the tree of the knowledge of good and evil. Edwards spends some time on Adam and Eve being "naked and unashamed," conjecturing, "It is no improbable conjecture that the bodies of our first Parents while in their state of innocence appeared with such a beauty and had such a luster and glory from head to feet that far more than supplied the want of garments."⁷⁶ Edwards says that Adam and Eve were clothed with a robe of light, similar to the way Moses' face shined.

When Adam and Eve sinned, they lost the beauty and luster of their bodies and became corrupted and deformed. God's continued rebuke of them reflected their heinousness in his sight. This leads Edwards to his doctrine, "The act of our first father in eating the forbidden fruit was a very

---

73. *WJEO* 54:504. Edwards dates the sermon Feb. 1738, but this is the Old Style calendar. The 1739 date used in the Master Sermon Index is New Style. Date citations will reflect this with "Feb 1738/39."

74. *WJE* 18: entry no. 788.

75. *WJE* 17:329–49.

76. *WJEO* 54:504.

heinous act."⁷⁷ Everyone, says Edwards, should consider the nature of that act of Adam since he is humanity's surety. This subject teaches about humanity's sin and secondly, the righteousness available through the second Adam. "It is of infinite importance that we should know both, for the first is our own, by which we are undone; and we must know the former in order to know the latter."⁷⁸

At this point in the sermon Edwards says there is a twofold heinousness that must be distinguished. The first heinousness is the act that concerns Adam personally, as it relates to his unique position. The second heinousness is in Adam's act as public head, and thus in all his posterity. Edwards laboriously makes the distinction between Adam's sin which was peculiar to him as a person and his sin which was imputed to his posterity. "Adam is guilty of murdering all his posterity by that act of sin. It is often mentioned as a great aggravation of that act of his, but it is not so carefully observed as it should be that this is something that peculiarly concerns Adam: an aggravation arising from his peculiar relations and not concerning his posterity."⁷⁹

One of the primary aspects of Adam's sin that was not imputed to his posterity was the guilt of murdering all his posterity by virtue of imputation. The imputation of sin is unique to Adam's sin. "This circumstance is peculiar to him alone and can't be reckoned to his posterity."⁸⁰ Adam's position as the public head of humanity, and the covenant of works made with Adam and his posterity, makes Adam's sin during his probation a unique sin. To be sure, Adam's transgression of disobedience and rebellion is imputed to his posterity. Edwards returns to the heinousness of Adam's sin, saying that the heinousness of the sin is that it was against the nature of God and against the nature of the covenant. Adam committed the ultimate treasonous act. Adam stood in the stead of all his posterity, he enjoyed fellowship with God, and by his disobedience, murdered his children. This first preaching unit is repetitive, and Edwards's focus is on the heinousness of Adam's sin as the public head representing his posterity in the covenant of works.

The second preaching unit picks up the twofold heinousness. Edwards seems to make sure every stone is turned over a few times. Edwards points out that Adam's sin was a sin of the heart, not just an overt act. The moment Adam began to listen to the temptation and his mind began to dwell on it, as he parleyed with the serpent, there was the beginning lust in his heart, which was conceived and then cherished. Then the overt act took place.

77. *WJEO* 54:504.
78. *WJEO* 54:504.
79. *WJEO* 54:504.
80. *WJEO* 54:504.

This overt act was a total violation of God's command. This was no sin of ignorance. Edwards acknowledges that sometimes "men blind themselves before they commit a sinful act."[81] Edwards asserts that was not the case with Adam, he was not blind nor was he ignorant. Adam had an express prohibition and he deliberately violated it, even though it was given with the greatest solemnity.

Edwards states the solemnity of the prohibition: "The command was enforced with threatening and denounced in a most awful preemptory manner."[82] Here Edwards appeals to the original Hebrew, as he explains the threat. In the original, says Edwards, "It is dying thou shalt die."[83] Edwards gives a grammatical insight into the phrase, pointing out that the repetition in Hebrew "denotes a superlative, so in the repetition the Holy of holies. signifies the most holy of all."[84] Edwards opens up the phrase "dying thou shalt die" as "the most dreadful death. All manner of death, not only death temporally, but spiritually and eternal. The highest and most dreadful thing that can be signified by the word death is everlasting misery and destruction."[85] Again, Edwards tediously teases out the idea of death and the subsequent punishment.

Edwards moves to another reason why Adam's sin was so heinous. Adam's sin was a violation against great encouragements for obedience and a glorious promise of eternal life. Adam's sin was not merely a flagrant act of defiance in the face of the worst possible threat, it was also a flagrant act of defiance in the face of the best possible promise. Additionally, Adam sinned in the perfect exercise of the freedom of his own will. No one since the time of Adam has ever sinned like Adam because all of Adam's posterity are already in a state of bondage to sin. Only Adam sinned with a perfectly free will. Adam was not dead in sin, but possessed an original righteousness, and according to Edwards, even had the Spirit of God dwelling in him.

Edwards continues his exploration of this aspect of Adam's sin. Adam had other commands, but the command not to eat was a special command manifesting God's authority. Although Edwards does not use the terminology, this prohibition was a case of positive law. This law, based on God's own pleasure, was broken by Adam with great ease. Adam was not starving; he was surrounded by plenty to eat. "He was rich in a great affluence of good things on every side. God had provided a great variety of excellent

---

81. *WJEO* 54:504.
82. *WJEO* 54:504.
83. *WJEO* 54:504.
84. *WJEO* 54:504.
85. *WJEO* 54:504.

and dainty food for him. Never was any prince feasted as Adam was before his fall."[86] The goodness of God to Adam only demonstrates the aggravated nature of Adam's sin against God. Adam enjoyed God's abundance, God's felicity, there was nothing that could trouble him, he lived in pleasant communion with his Creator. Adam's existence "was filled with nothing but Gods smiles."[87] Adam's sin was against light and knowledge and so its heinousness was that it was committed with deliberation. It was a horrible act of unbelief, listening to the devil when he suggested God lied. Adam's sin was an act of base ingratitude. All of this was conceived in Adam's heart, but it was the external deed which ruined him and his posterity.

In the third preaching unit, Edwards acknowledges his tedious exposition when he says, "This act has been particularly insisted on."[88] Edwards has shown the heinousness of Adam's sin, which concerned him personally, and the heinousness of the act which was equally imputed to him and his posterity. But then Edwards tells his listeners that before he gets to the application, he wants to answer the question, "Why that first act of sin in our father Adam [his eating the forbidden fruit] is imputed to his posterity and not other sins that he committed afterwards."[89] At this point in the discourse on Gen 3:11, Edwards has piled argument upon argument. There is a monotony in the first two preaching units, and there is a lack of vivid, gripping imagery, not to mention typological exposition. These units are polemical, building a case regarding the nature of Adam's sin. Edwards continues this approach in the third preaching unit, as he defends the imputation of Adam's sin. Edwards asks the question, "Now thereof what can be the reason of this, why other sins of our common head and father Adam, and others breaches of the Covenant of Works that he was guilty of, should not be imputed to us as well as that first sin."[90] Edwards's answer is straightforward: the time of Adam's trials as the covenant head of his posterity was over as soon as Adam violated the one command to not eat of the tree of the knowledge of good and evil. The command was the probation period, and when he disobeyed the probation was over and he no longer acted as the public head of the human race.

Edwards illustrates this point by using Jesus Christ, the second Adam. Edwards asserts that Christ's obedience, which he performed during his time of trial, is what is imputed to believers for justification. Christ is still

86. *WJEO* 54:504.
87. *WJEO* 54:504.
88. *WJEO* 54:504.
89. *WJEO* 54:504.
90. *WJEO* 54:504.

obedient to the Father in heaven right now (1 Cor 15:28), but his subsequent post-ascension acts of obedience are not what is imputed to his people. Once the sentence of justification has been passed at the resurrection, his state of probation was over, he entered the state of his reward. The same holds true of the first Adam. Adam's subsequent sins, after his failed probation, only affected him.

The application begins halfway through this third preaching unit. Edwards's first application is that his hearers must learn how guilty they are as they entered this world. Adam's sin was the sin of all his posterity. However, Edwards also notes that Adam's innocency and righteousness also belonged to them as well. And just as certainly as Adam willfully and deliberately broke God's command, so also Edwards's listeners violate God's commands every time they exercise the vile lust of sensuality. Edwards says of himself and his congregation that just like Adam, they had cast off God's authority, apostatized from God, and turned into his enemies. Edwards says, "we are guilty of that horrid ingratitude, perfidiousness, presumption, and folly, that was in that act."[91]

Edwards then defends the concept of imputation. In what appears to be a deviation from the application, Edwards shows that covenant transaction includes the seed or posterity of the one with whom the covenant is made. Edwards uses the covenants with Noah, Abraham, Phinehas, and David to prove his point. Edwards continues building his case of imputation by appealing to experience and observation, and the death of infants. If Adam's posterity was not included in Adam as covenant head, then mankind is not fallen. For those who object to imputation, they must consider that the righteousness of Christ is imputed to them under the same principle.

Edwards departs from the application in the third unit of this discourse and reverts again to defending imputation. In the fourth sermon he somewhat resumes the application by driving home the dreadful loss humanity has experienced because of Adam's fall. Again, Edwards is repetitive. Edwards speaks of having lost the image of God, deprived of the excellency and beauty of the original righteousness. The robe of light, which shined in Adam and Eve, has turned to deformity. Furthermore, man lost sweet, pleasant communion with God. Because Adam tasted the forbidden fruit, all the pleasant blessings were lost, and "a kind of darkness was introduced on all things here below."[92] As in the Gen 3:24 sermon, Edwards expounds the loss of eternal life and happiness in the fall. Although his language is not nearly as gripping and vivid, he does employ some of the same imagery.

91. *WJEO* 54:504.
92. *WJEO* 54:504.

The consequences of the fall on humanity fall into two main categories: sin and suffering. Sin exercises dominion and power over Adam's fallen race. Humanity now has an aversion to that which is good and a proneness to all that is evil. The worst consequence of the fall, but a necessary one, was God leaving man's heart, where he had dwelled. Man, as it were, drove God's Spirit out of his heart by his rebellion. This divine abandonment left man in a totally corrupt state.

Edwards then asks the question of transmission, "how the corruption of nature comes to be transmitted from father to son."[93] Edwards admits that this is a much-disputed topic but appeals to the covenant that God made with Adam. If it were not for the covenant arrangement neither guilt nor corruption would have been derived from Adam. The covenant of works was made with Adam and his posterity, and so there is no need to postulate any farther on how the guilt is transmitted.

The second consequence is suffering. Edwards notes, "All sufferings are natural evils, both in this world and that which is to come. Mankind are subject to the consequences."[94] Edwards points out that all suffering and all misery, from infancy to old age, for rich and poor, come from the fall. The grave is a constant reminder of the reign of sin and death. The dreadfulness of the consequences is seen in their nature and degree, the hand of the devil in them, as well as the extent and duration of them. All eternity will testify to heinousness of Adam's fall and mankind's sins.

Edwards concludes, "Since the rebellion of our first surety was so heinous, what cause have we to admire the grace of God in giving his own Son to be our second Adam."[95] In this final section Edwards extols the Lord Jesus Christ in his superlative excellency. If the first Adam's sin was heinous, the grace of God in the second Adam is infinitely more glorious. The second Adam is the only begotten of the Father, the dearly beloved Son, the King of Heaven, and the Lord of Angels. The first Adam was a mere creature who faced an easy trial. The trial of the second Adam was exceedingly difficult by comparison, and he conquered Satan. The first Adam only had to obey one easy command. The second Adam had to obey the Law and suffer the punishment for sin. Edwards employs similar language from previous sermons, but the language soars. Edwards is incredibly fond of the restoration motif: what Adam ruined Christ has restored. But Christ's restoration was not merely restoration to the original state, rather it is "to a much higher

---

93. *WJEO* 54:504.
94. *WJEO* 54:504.
95. *WJEO* 54:504.

pitch of happiness."⁹⁶ Christ procures a much greater reward by his obedience than Adam could have ever attained by his.

God gave a promise that he was going to save men through the second Adam. Edwards, in a glimpse of exegetical insight, notes, "Eve seems to express her faith in that promise from time-to-time Gen 4:1."⁹⁷ This understanding of Gen 4:1 is predicated on a point of Hebrew grammar. The AV reads, "And Adam knew Eve his wife; and she conceived, and bare Cain, and said, I have gotten a man from the LORD." The Hebrew text reads, "I have gotten a man, the LORD." There is a direct object or accusative marker preceding the divine name. This would mean that Eve's hope was messianic, shaped by Gen 3:15.⁹⁸

Edwards finally does apply the sermon. This text is a warning to people not to fall into heinous sin like their first parents. The warning is to "beware lest we are drawn away by that same tempter—2. Cor. 11:3."⁹⁹ Edwards urges his congregation to stop all communication with the tempter. This means being aware of the instruments the devil uses, like companions or even best friends. Christians need to do better than their first parents in that they look to God and depend on him for strength, not on themselves, like Adam and Eve. Edwards urges, "Let all earnestly seek that we may be the children of the second Adam."¹⁰⁰

This discourse in four sermons is unlike Edwards's other Genesis sermons. First, there is a tremendous amount of tedious and even repetitive argumentation regarding the imputation of Adam's sin. Although there are some mild typological inferences, such as "Adam is a negative example," this is far from a major aspect of the sermon. Second, there is very little application. Even in the section identified as application, Edwards gets off track quickly and reverts to more arguments regarding imputation. Edwards's polemics regarding original sin and the freedom of the will come much later in his career. It appears that these four sermons reflect more of Edwards's own theological musings as he prepared for his grand project on the history of redemption.

In summary, Edwards's preaching from 1736–1739 reflects both the stressful pastoral situations he had been encountering as well as his own personal biblical interests. The period picks up with the end of the Connecticut

---

96. *WJEO* 54:504.

97. *WJEO* 54:504.

98. "See the reasons given why this should have been translated, 'I have gotten a man, the Lord,' i.e., the Messiah. Poole's *Synopsis, in locum*, place marked in margin." *WJE* 24:141.

99. *WJEO* 54:504.

100. *WJEO* 54:504.

Valley revival (ca. 1735–1737), which Edwards had written about in glowing terms in *A Faithful Narrative of the Surprising Work of God* (published in London in 1737). During this period, the matriarch Mrs. Stoddard died, his sister Lucy died, a new building project had been approved, and the old meetinghouse gallery had collapsed. As revival fires died out, old rivalries and arrogant attitudes were resurrected, and there were serious issues of immorality among the young people. Edwards's two sermons on Genesis 28 represent both his expanding emphasis on typological interests, and strong pastoral application. Nevertheless, what is also seen in this same period is a strong emphasis on exemplary, hortatory, applicatory preaching. This is demonstrated most clearly in his Abraham and Joseph sermons, where there is very little typology and an abundance of application. The Gen 12:2 sermon seems to reflect a degree of frustration, indicated in the excessively long and repetitious application. Finally, at the end of this period Edwards's sermon on Gen 3:11 seems wholly dedicated preparation for his larger "Redemption Discourse" project. In comparison with his earlier period (1727–1735), Edwards does dive deeper into more abstract theology and more detailed typology, while not neglecting strong pastoral preaching.

Chapter Five

Edwards's Use of Genesis in *A History of the Work of Redemption*

HAVING EXPLORED IN THE preceding chapters specific sermons on Genesis of Edwards's Northampton years 1727–1739, attention is now turned to the use of the book of Genesis in a particular sermon series of Edwards's, the "Redemption Discourse." Following the Connecticut Valley revival of ca. 1735–1737, Edwards noticed a spiritual and moral backsliding in his congregation. And thus, he embarked on preaching various sermon series (On the Parable of the Wise and Foolish Virgins, On Charity and Its Fruits), including a history of the work of redemption, the "Redemption Discourse," In this extended sermon series, Edwards used the book of Genesis widely.

Edwards had a vision for a "new method" of looking at the Bible and theology. The new method was historical and theological. Edwards's work on this vision began with a series of thirty sermons, preached from Isa 51:8. The series extended from March until August of 1739. John F. Wilson notes, "Jonathan Edwards's *A History of the Work of Redemption* stands apart in the body of his writings. We know that he intended to bring his thought to its summation in a volume which would give theology a new basis in the theme of God's redemption of the world."[1]

1. *WJE* 9:1.

Edwards's *Work of Redemption* was a project which occupied much of his attention. Edwards makes mention of this project to the College of New Jersey board of trustees. The letter is dated October 19, 1757.

> But besides these, I have had on my mind and heart (which I long ago began, not with any view to publication) a great work, which I call *A History of the Work of Redemption*, a body of divinity in an entire new method, being thrown into the form of an history, considering the affair of Christian theology, as the whole of it, in each part, stands in reference to the great work of redemption by Jesus Christ; which I suppose is to be the grand design of all God's designs, and the *summum* and *ultimum* of all the divine operations and degrees; particularly considering all parts of the grand scheme in their historical order.[2]

The project was mentioned in correspondence with John Erskine during Edwards's Stockbridge years.[3] There are also three notebooks, analyzed by Wilson, which reflect Edwards's continued work on this project.[4] The sermons Edwards preached from Isa 51:8, almost two decades earlier, appear to be the beginnings of this "new method" of divinity. "From the outset Edwards clearly looked on 'The Redemption Discourse' as an endeavor unlike any he had attempted before."[5] Unfortunately, Edwards never completed his grand project. Edwards's "fatal choice"[6] of going to Princeton instead of finishing his project would leave his heirs only with the sermons from Isa 51:8 and his notebooks. These sermons would be published posthumously as *A History of the Work of Redemption* in Scotland in 1774.[7]

What made Edwards's initial efforts new was its redemptive-historical approach. It would probably be a mistake to think of Edwards's "new method," mentioned in the trustee letter, simply as an expansion on the 1739 sermons. McDermott and McClymond point out, "Yet the reference to a 'new body of divinity in an entire [sic] new method' suggests something quite different from the sermons. Edwards knew very well what 'body

2. *WJE* 16:727–28.
3. *WJE* 9:11–12.
4. *WJE* 9:543–56.
5. *WJE* 9:9. Wilson uses "Redemption Discourse" for the 1739 sermon series.
6. Lucas, "History of the Work of Redemption," 176. The "fatal choice" refers to the move to Princeton, which resulted in Edwards receiving the smallpox vaccination that led to his death.
7. *WJE* 9:20–28, "The Publication of the Redemption Discourse." The editorial process of this publication is unclear, with both Jonathan Edwards Jr. and John Erskine having a hand in it. The text of the sermons, however, in the Yale edition is based on the transcription of the original sermons.

of divinity; signifies, and in theology this connotes a whole composed of interdependent part."[8] While that seems to be accurate, the 1739 sermon series was at least seminal in Edwards's approach. The discourse was based on one text, Isa 51:8, "for the moth shall them up like a garment, and the worm shall eat them like wool; but my righteousness shall be forever, and my salvation from generation to the generation." Edwards exegetes his text by giving the context of the chapter, which is the comfort and consolation of the church under persecution and suffering. The consolation is God's mercy and faithfulness in continuing the work of salvation for her. Edwards then points out that the promise is, "1. How short-lived the power and prosperity of the church's enemies is."[9] Edwards then moves to "2. The contrary happy lot and portion of God's church expressed in these words, 'my righteousness shall be forever and my salvation [from generation to generation].'"[10] Edwards argues in his exegesis of "my righteousness" that the phrase refers to "God's covenant faithfulness." Edwards sees "salvation" as the effect of God's righteousness. Finally, he exegetes the phrase "from generation to generation." "It is from generation to generation, i.e., throughout all generations beginning with the generations of men on the earth and not ending till these generations end at the end of the world."[11] Edwards's exegesis of Isa 51:8 is thorough and argued primarily through the use of cross-referencing proof texts.

The doctrine deduced from the text was that "the work of redemption is a work that God carries on from the fall of man to the end of the world."[12] The work of redemption is "all that is wrought in the execution of the eternal Covenant of Redemption. This is what I called the work of redemption in the doctrine, for it is all but one work, one design."[13] This work of redemption is carried on from the fall of man to the end of the world. The goal of this work is the restoration of all things in Christ, to the glory of the blessed Trinity.[14] This work is accomplished in various stages. Edwards sees three stages. The first is from the fall to the incarnation of Christ. This stage is preparatory for the coming of Christ. The second is from the incarnation to the resurrection of Christ, "or the whole time of his humiliation."[15] This

8. McClymond and McDermott, *Theology of Jonathan Edwards*, 184–85.
9. *WJE* 9:113.
10. *WJE* 9:114.
11. *WJE* 9:116.
12. *WJE* 9:116.
13. *WJE* 9:118.
14. This is a summary of the first sermon.
15. *WJE* 9:127.

stage is the purchase of redemption. The third stage is from the resurrection to the end of the world. This stage brings about "accomplishing the great effect or success of that purchase."[16]

Edwards says there are six subsections to the first stage; the first three are from the fall to the flood, from the flood to Abraham, from Abraham to Moses. The book of Genesis is especially relevant to the first three subsets since it covers that span of redemptive history. Edwards will use many of the early chapters of Genesis in his sermons on the first stage and the first three subsets. However, for the purpose of this study, we will examine Edwards's use of Gen 3:15 and its context as the first gospel promise, and then Abraham, Jacob, and Joseph. Genesis 3:15 cannot be exaggerated as a critical text in Edwards's thinking. "Edwards was firmly within his theological tradition in beginning with this Genesis text. Van Mastricht, for example, not only began with this text, but he used Genesis 3:15 as the foundational text for his entire chapter on *De Foedere Gratiae*."[17] Although brief observations about the use of other Genesis texts will be made along the way for context, this narrower selection will roughly correspond to Edwards's Genesis sermons.

Edwards notes that "Christ began to exercise the office of mediator between God and man as soon as man fell because mercy began to be exercised towards man immediately."[18] Edwards says that "the gospel was first revealed on the earth in these words, Genesis 3:15, 'And I will put enmity between three and the woman, [and between thy seed and her seed; it shall bruise thy head].'"[19] It is here that Edwards begins to employ Genesis by focusing on the first gospel promise. Genesis 3:15 plays a large role in this first stage. It is the dawning of the light of the gospel after the darkness of the fall. Edwards sees Gen 3:15 as the revelation of the covenant of grace, and in that promise God slays beasts in order to provide a covering for Adam and Eve. Edwards sees in this slaying and covering a type of Christ:

> So does Christ, to afford clothing for our naked souls; the skin signifies the life. . . . Thus our first parents were covered with skins of the sacrifice, as the tabernacle in the wilderness, which

16. *WJE* 9:128.

17. Bogue, *Jonathan Edwards and the Covenant of Grace*, 118. Edwards's use of Gen 3:15 as the first promise of the covenant of grace, and the promise of the coming Redeemer, make Gen 3:15 and its immediate context indispensable in this analysis. Edwards exegetes Gen 3:15 and mentions it or alludes to it eight times in the first three sermons. Edwards's prior use of Abraham, Jacob, and Joseph in his sermons makes a comparison with his uses of these OT persons in the "Redemption Discourse" provides important observations on Edwards's versatile exegetical methods.

18. *WJE* 9:130.

19. *WJE* 9:132.

signified the church, was when it was covered with ram's skins dyed red as though they were dipped in blood, to signify that Christ's righteousness was wrought out through the pains of death which he shed his precious blood.[20]

That this promise was embraced by Adam and Eve is supported by Edwards's use of an exegetical insight which he had gleaned from his four-part sermon from Gen 3:11 when he explains Eve's hope in Gen 4:1.[21]

> Eve seems plainly to express her hope in and dependence on that promise in what she says in the birth of Cain, Genesis 4:1 ["I have gotten a man from the Lord"], i.e., as God has promised my seed should [bruise the serpent's head], so now has God given me this pledge and token of it that I have a seed born. She plainly owns that this her child is from God and hoped that her promised seed was to be of this her eldest son, though she was mistaken.[22]

In the first two sermons of "The Redemption Discourse," Edwards relies heavily on the messianic understanding of the promise on Gen 3:15.[23] The messianic understanding is typological in that the seed of the woman finds it ultimate fulfillment in Jesus Christ and his saving work. The promise of the gospel, or covenant of grace, is given to Adam and Eve, and they are saved by this promise. Adam and Eve trust God's promise, God slays animals to cover their nakedness, which Edwards also understands typologically as the atoning work of Christ. Finally, Edwards, as he did in his previous Genesis sermons, interprets Eve's statement in Gen 4:1 as her messianic hope, albeit mistaken.[24]

The third sermon continues the preparatory stage, beginning with Enoch. Edwards sees the days of Enoch as a great outpouring of the Spirit (Gen 4:26). After the days of Enoch "the church of God greatly diminished."[25] Edwards understands the "sons of God" in Gen 6:1–2 as the godly line of Seth, and their intermarriage with daughters of men as an indication of the

---

20. *WJE* 9:136.

21. Cf. pp. 74–75.

22. *WJE* 9:138–39.

23. Edwards cites Arthur Bedford's *Scripture Chronology* on this text in his "Blank Bible," "which shows that by 'seed' is meant a particular person and not her posterity in general." *WJE* 24:128.

24. "In Eve's expressing herself so, it is probable she had an eye to what God said, that her seed should break the serpent's head [Gen 3:15]; for now, seeing she had a son, her faith and hope was strengthened that the promise should be fulfilled." *WJE* 15:74.

25. *WJE* 9:147.

degeneration of the church. God's work of redemption continues during those days by God bringing judgment through the flood. The flood not only brings judgment on the wicked, but it is also salvation for the church. Edwards's exegesis of the flood is heavily typological: "That water that washed away the filth of the world, that cleared the world of wicked men, was a type of the blood of Christ that takes away the sin of the world."[26] The covenant God makes with Noah and his family, according to Edwards, was a renewal of the covenant of grace.

Against the background of the idolatry of Babel, Edwards begins his exposition of Abraham. For Edwards, Abraham is a pivotal person in the history of redemption. First, God separates Abraham out of his idolatrous country and kindred in order to preserve the church for the coming of Christ. God is doing a new thing with Abraham. God is building the foundation for upholding the church until Christ should come. "There was a necessity that the seed of the woman should thus be separated from the idolatrous world in order to that."[27] God also gave a fuller revelation of the covenant of grace to Abraham. God gave the sign and seal of the covenant in circumcision. Edwards sees further confirmation of the covenant of grace when Abraham encounters Melchizedek in Genesis 14. Melchizedek is a type of Christ and the bread and wine which he offered signified the bread and wine in the Lord's Supper.[28] Edwards sees both circumcision and Melchizedek's offerings as pointing to the two Christian sacraments ordained by Christ, namely, baptism and the Lord's Supper.

Edwards treats the covenant confirmation of Genesis 15 as christological. The sacrifices which were cut in two signify the sacrifice of Christ. The smoking furnace that passes through the sacrifices typifies Christ's sufferings.[29] It is interesting to observe that the most profoundly typological passage in the Abraham narrative, the offering of Isaac in Genesis 22, is

---

26. *WJE* 9:151.
27. *WJE* 9:159.
28. *WJE* 24:157.
29. "Here were four things that were significant of the death and last sufferings of Christ, all at the same time. 1. There were the sacrifices that were slain and lay there, dead and divided. Christ feared when his last passion approached, lest Satan should utterly devour him, and swallow him up in that trial, and cried to God, and was heard in that he feared; and those fowls were frayed away that sought to devour that sacrifice, as Abraham frayed away the fowls that attempted to devour this sacrifice while it lay upon the altar [Gen 15:11]. 2. The smoking furnace that passed through the midst of the sacrifices. 3. The 'deep sleep that fell upon Abraham,' and the 'horror of great darkness' that fell upon him [Gen 15:11]. 4. The sun, that greatest of all natural types of Christ, went down and descended under the earth, and it was dark." *WJE* 15: 339–40.

treated minimally by Edwards. Edwards does reference Heb 11:17–19, but basically focuses on this event as a confirmation of the covenant.

> Thus you see how much more fully the Covenant of Grace was revealed and confirmed in Abraham's time than ever it had been before, by means of which Abraham seems to have had a more clear understanding and sight of Christ the great Redeemer and the future things that were to be accomplished by him than any of the saints that had gone before had had.[30]

When Edwards preached on Abraham from Gen 12:12 in June of 1737, the sermon was almost wholly ethical. There was not much emphasis on Abraham as a type of the believer. In Edwards's treatment of Abraham in "The Redemption Discourse," there is also very little typology applied to Abraham. Abraham is seen in his redemptive historical significance; he is a pivotal figure in terms of preparation for the coming of Christ and for the notable advance in the revelation of the covenant of grace. The christological typology Edwards does appeal to is Melchizedek and the malediction oath of Genesis 15.

After expounding on Abraham, Edwards makes some passing comments about the patriarchs and how God protected them from the wickedness of the world. Edwards points out that the destruction of Sodom and Gomorrah was an important event in the history of redemption because it made visible God's judgment against sin. The destruction of Sodom and Gomorrah was a future picture of the misery and suffering of the wicked.

Edwards next section focuses on God renewing the covenant of grace to Isaac and Jacob. Isaac is barely mentioned. However, when Edwards deals with Jacob, he draws much on his sermon from Gen 28:12, dated March 1736. This was one of Edwards's most typologically oriented sermons from Genesis, and it echoes in "The Redemption Discourse." Edwards is concise. The ladder was a symbol of the way of salvation by Christ. The stone Jacob rested his head was a type of Christ. This stone of Israel was a type of Christ because it was anointed by Jacob and turned into an altar. "But we know that Christ is the anointed of God and is the only true altar of God."[31] What Edwards sees in this is that the covenant of grace is being renewed with greater frequency. "The light of the gospel now began to shine much brighter as the time drew nearer that Christ should come."[32]

Edwards's exegesis of Jacob relies much on his previous Genesis sermon and was rich in typology. Edwards foregoes any mention of Genesis

---

30. *WJE* 9:165.
31. *WJE* 9:170.
32. *WJE* 9:170.

32 and Jacob's wrestling with the angel of God. That passage, although rich in typology, especially with Jacob as the believer, was not germane to Edwards's argument. Edwards clearly thought the event at Bethel was more covenantally and christologically significant.

The preservation of the patriarchs is still in view when Edwards arrives at the Joseph narrative. "The next thing I would observe is God's so remarkably preserving the family of Christ of which Christ was to proceed from perishing by famine by the instrumentality of Joseph."[33] In one densely packed paragraph, Edwards piles up the type and ante-type between Joseph and Jesus.[34] First, Joseph was sent into Egypt to save the holy seed. Edwards observes how many times the glorious Redeemer was in danger of being destroyed, but God always preserved him. Edwards then makes this observation: "This salvation of the house of Israel by Joseph was upon many accounts very much a semblance of the salvation of Christ."[35]

First, the children of Jacob were saved from famine by a near kinsman and brother. Jesus saves the souls of spiritual Israel from spiritual famine, as their kinsman. Joseph was hated and sold by his brothers and they designed to kill him. So, too, human beings hate Christ and by their wicked lives have sold him for the vanities of this world, and by their sins, they have slain Jesus. Joseph was first in a state of humiliation and was a servant. So Christ appeared in the form of a servant and went into the dungeon of the grave. Christ arose and then entered his state of exaltation, just as Joseph was exalted to the king's right hand.[36] Just as Joseph saved the lives of those who hated him, so Christ gives the gift of salvation to rebels who hate him.

In "The Redemption Discourse" he gives only a very cursory overview. In both the "Blank Bible" and "Miscellanies" no. 1069, known as "Types of Messiah," Edwards pushes the Joseph typologies as far as possible.[37] In "Types of Messiah," Edwards makes some basic connections between Joseph and Christ, for instance both are "beloved sons." Both are hated by their brothers, and are saviors not only of their brothers, but also the world.

---

33. *WJE* 9:170–71.

34. Edwards preached in Feb. 1742, sermon 651, "Joseph was a remarkable type of Christ," from Gen 43:3.

35. *WJE* 9:171.

36. "By Joseph's being cast into the dungeon is signified the death of Christ; by his being delivered, his resurrection; and the ensuing great advancement of Joseph, to be next to the king, signifies the exaltation of Christ at the right hand of the Father. Joseph rose from the dungeon, and was thus exalted, to give salvation to the land of Egypt and to his brethren, as Christ to save his people." *WJE* 15:86.

37. *WJE* 24:187–204. *WJE* 11:228–37. In his coverage of Gen 37–50 in the "Blank Bible," Edwards cites Matthew Henry twice and Matthew Poole's *Synopsis* fourteen times.

But then Edwards goes beyond the obvious. Joseph was clothed with a beautiful garment, "So the prophecies represent the Messiah as clothed with beautiful and glorious garments."[38] Edwards peels back layers in the text as he uncovers the types. The sheaves bowing down to Joseph point to Christ, who is the firstborn king of all the earth. The sun, moon, and stars bowing down to Joseph point to Messiah, "whom the Old Testament often speaks of as ruling sun, moon and stars."[39] This also symbolizes Messiah's ancestors worshiping him.

Edwards appeals to etymology for some typological insight. Joseph's Egyptian name, "Zaphanth-paaneah," according to Edwards, means "the savior of the world."[40] But then Edwards says Joseph was a prophet. "He was a revealed of secrets, as his name, 'Zaphanath-paaneah,' signifies in the Hebrew tongue."[41] Joseph's wife name was "Asenath," "which signifies 'an unfortunate thing.' Agreeable to this, the Messiah is represented as espousing, after his exaltation, a poor, unhappy, afflicted disconsolate creature."[42]

There are other typological interpretations in the "Blank Bible" which are not in "Types of Messiah." For instance, "Joseph's coat being dipped in the blood of a kid was probably ordered in providence to point forth Jesus Christ, the antitype of Joseph, the Lamb that was slain, the great antitype of the paschal lamb, and of the lamb of the daily sacrifice, and all other lambs that were offered in sacrifice to God."[43] The good of all the land of Egypt (Gen 45:20) is the heavenly treasure Christ offers his people.[44] There are many others that could be cited; however, it becomes clear that in "The

---

38. *WJE* 11:228.

39. *WJE* 11:239. In the "Blank Bible," Edwards notes, "Joseph's dreaming that the sun, moon, and stars made obeisance to him has respect to something beyond his father, and mother, and brethren bowing to him. It has respect to all things, not only in earth but in heaven, being put in subjection to Christ, and in him to the church, so that all shall be theirs, and they shall reign over all." *WJE* 24:187.

40. *WJE* 11:231.

41. *WJE* 11:231–32. In the "Blank Bible," Edwards expands this theme. "When the king exalted Joseph, he gave him a new name. So Christ in the Revelation speaks of his new name, by which is meant that new honor and glory which he received at his exaltation. Joseph's new name, '*Zaphnath-paaneah*,' signifies 'revealer of secrets' [Gen 41:45]. Christ was the greater revealer of secrets, *John 1:18*, who came out of 'the bosom of the Father,' and was the great prophet of God, to bring to life mysteries that had been kept secret since the world began. Some translate Joseph's new name, 'the savior of the world.' See SSS." *WJE* 24:194.

42. *WJE* 11:234.

43. *WJE* 24:187.

44. *WJE* 24:196.

Redemption Discourse" Edwards exercised great restraint in his typological understanding of the Joseph narrative.

In "The Redemption Discourse," the final chapters of Genesis represent the end of the first subsection of the first stage of the history of redemption. In his closing remarks, he points out the prophecy in Gen 49:8–9, demonstrating that the promise and predictions are narrowing the limits of Abraham's posterity for the promised seed, that is Christ.[45] He concludes this fourth sermon, "Thus you see how that gospel light dawned immediately after the fall of man gradually increases."[46]

As Edwards moves through these first four sermons of his grand project, covering the span of the book of Genesis in redemptive history, one notices that he does not strictly follow his preaching pattern. In these first four sermons he has yet to make application. It is not until sermon 13 that he begins with "Improvement." Edwards will start sermon 25 the same way, "Having now shown how the work of redemption has been carried on from the fall of man to the present time, before I proceed any further, I would make some, improvement."[47] Sermons 29 and 30 contain, "Application of the whole."[48]

It seems that "The Redemption Discourse" was, in Edwards's mind, one lengthy exposition of the history of redemption with a text and a doctrine, while the preaching units seem somewhat inconsequential to Edwards. Although he covers various epochs of redemptive history with relative brevity, he is not interested in the patriarchs as patterns for believers nor for pastoral applications. Edwards was interested in setting forth the pivotal moments, both in terms of the unfolding of the covenant of grace and typologies of Christ which are preparatory for the second stage, from the advent of Christ to his resurrection. When comparing his typological understanding of this portion of Genesis with "The Redemption Discourse" sermons and his "Blank Bible" and "Types of Messiah," Edwards's sermons were not designed to explore every detail, but to give an overview. Edwards sees Genesis as literal history, theological or redemptive history, and as covenantally and typologically foundational for the rest of Scripture and history.

---

45. Edwards in the "Blank Bible" goes into great typological detail in the Gen 49 passage, again showing his restraint in the "Redemption Discourse". *WJE* 24:198–205.

46. *WJE* 9:172.

47. *WJE* 9:442.

48. *WJE* 9:510–28.

A PRELIMINARY ASSESSMENT OF EDWARDS'S SERMONS ON GENESIS: 1727–1735, 1736–1739, AND THE "REDEMPTION DISCOURSE"

Following the discussion of the use of the book of Genesis in the "Redemption Discourse," it seems appropriate at this point to assess this review with the sermons preached on Genesis during the periods of 1727–1735 and 1736–1739. The question is whether there is anything observable in identifying Edwards's exegetical method in preaching Genesis to his congregation. Did Edwards have a consistent approach in the way he handled the texts from which he would base his sermons? How does Edwards the exegete shape Edwards the preacher? The first observation is that Edwards's labor takes place within the context of a local church and community. Edwards the exegete is an exegete in a context, a context where suicide, death of prominent people, calamities, and sins dominate the landscape. One cannot consider Edwards's handling the biblical texts in Genesis apart from the stresses, concerns, and issues of a real pastor.

The second observation is that Edwards demonstrates no observable consistent exegetical method in preparing sermons for his congregation. Edwards was consistent in his structure and never failed to give the historical setting of the text before stating the doctrine. But in the body of his Genesis sermons, Edwards appears very occasional, that is, there is a pastoral pragmatism as he approaches the text. This pastoral focus shaped much of what Edwards did with the text. Sometimes he approached the texts from various levels of typology, but not as a mere typologist. There are two classifications of Edwards's typology in his sermons. The first and most basic is the historical persons in Genesis are types of the believer, whether Abraham, or more poignantly, Jacob or Joseph. This could be classified as exemplary-typology.

Edwards also interpreted the text typologically regarding the person and work of Christ. This second classification could be christological-typology. The christological focus is consistent in many of Edwards's sermons, whether it was Jacob's wrestling opponent, the ladder, or the last Adam. Although Edwards is generally restrained in his typology in his sermons, in at least one sermon, he pursued typological details. There is a noticeable difference between Edwards's exegetical reflections, for instance in the "Blank Bible," and his sermons. The typological use of Scripture is governed by pastoral and practical concerns. Even the stone as a type of Christ at Bethel is applied to believers to compel them to trust Christ.

Edwards on occasion also made theological use of Genesis. This is especially true when it came to Genesis 3 and the theological issues of the

Edwards's Use of Genesis in *A History of the Work of Redemption* 75

covenant of works, the imputation of Adam's sin, original sin, and redemption and restoration in Christ. In "East of Eden," for instance, there is rich theological depth, clothed with Edwards's vivid imagery and gripping language. Even theology needed to be preached in a way that enlightened and moved the congregation.

Edwards the busy and concerned pastor was still however, the obsessed student of Scripture, and on occasion this comes out. For instance, in the last Genesis sermon on Gen 3:11 there were polemical features to the sermon, such as the details of the imputation of Adam's sin, that one finds hard to imagine that the congregation was much concerned about. This sermon appears to be the fruit of Edwards's own theological interests as he prepared for his grand "Redemption Discourse." Nevertheless, Edwards demonstrates his theological exegesis, especially his commitment to Covenant Theology, as he expounds Genesis.

One of the strongest features of Edwards's use of Genesis was the applicatory or ethical use. Edwards skillfully used the characters of Genesis in an exemplary manner, but the application was driven by pastoral concerns that were going on in his congregation. Edwards's application at times could be wholly evangelistic, at other times it could be wholly ethical or moral. There is a strong pastoral pragmatism at times in Edwards's preaching, shaped by the concerns he had for his congregation for certain situations. Again, to miss these influences on Edwards is to miss an important dimension of him as an exegete and expositor.

One final observation is that Edwards appealed consistently to both reason and the senses. Edwards rigorously addressed the understanding or the reason. Edwards's exposition or application was filled with persuasive arguments. The argumentation addressed to the mind is unmistakable. But Edwards also spoke directly to the conscience. The Northampton pastor knew how to ask the convicting questions and how to use vivid language and imagery to move the affections. For Edwards, the text not only needed to be understood, but also felt. The job of the interpreter, therefore, was not only to bring out the historical meaning of the text and draw forth the doctrinal implications, but also to explain and apply those truths in a way that one sensed the power of the truth.

All three major works on Edwards as an exegete, considered earlier, make helpful and accurate observations about Edwards. Nichols's argument that Edwards's emphasis falls upon the dual authorship of Scripture and the necessity of the Spirit to see the divine intent is certainly true. Sweeney's assertion that Edwards was eclectic and did not have a uniform approach is supported in the variety of hermeneutical and homiletical approaches Edwards takes in Genesis. Barshinger's argument that Edwards is predominantly redemptive-historical, with a typological emphasis on Christ and the church also has merit. However, this overview of Edwards's sermons from Genesis reveals that Edwards was preeminently a pastor and he frequently used the Bible in a practical way. Perhaps the missing note in these major assessments is that Edwards regularly used Scripture in an exemplary manner, with a strong emphasis on ethics and application. Even Edwards's typology is regularly exemplary in application. Certainly, no one denies Edwards was an applicatory preacher—this was after all the all-important part of his inherited sermon structure. However, Edwards the exegete is Edwards the pastor, and thus he was a pastoral exegete. This does not mean that Edwards was not also the creative typologist or a nuanced theologian, for he was. But the missing note in many of the analyses is that Edwards frequently handled the text in a situational and strongly exemplary manner with an ethical emphasis, driven by pastoral concerns.

PART TWO

Theological

Chapter Six

Edwards's Theology of Man in the Image of God

"During the post-Reformation era, both English Puritans and Dutch Reformed theologians continued to display a strong commitment to the Reformation hermeneutical recalibration back to the literal tradition. To a man it appears they held to a creation *ex nihilo* and viewed the days of creation as ordinary due to the markers of evening and morning."[1] This was Edwards's inherited interpretive view of Genesis. However, Edwards's inheritance of a literal interpretation of the early chapters of Genesis was not without rivals. The Enlightenment brought new challenges to the foundational theological issues of Genesis. In response, vigorous defenses of the orthodox position of a literal creation and historical Adam were mounted by the Reformed Orthodox.[2] However, in colonial New England, Cotton Mather (1663–1728) represented those who were willing to tentatively consider the nonliteral reading of Genesis 1–2. "Thus, while Mather's thought reflected both accommodation to and criticism of nonliteral trends, this leading New England Puritan failed to exert a significant influence during his lifetime regarding theories of Genesis in British colonial North America."[3]

---

1. VanDoodewaard, *Quest for the Historical Adam*, 85.
2. VanDoodewaard, *Quest for the Historical Adam*, 95–116.
3. VanDoodewaard, *Quest for the Historical Adam*, 117.

Others in colonial New England took up the cause to defend the early chapters of Genesis. Benjamin Colman (1673–1747) was an influential pastor in Boston. Colman would maintain a wide correspondence with pastors and theologians in his day, including Jonathan Edwards.[4] In 1735 Colman wrote, *A Brief Dissertation on the Three First Chapters of Genesis*. Colman had the "Deists and Infidels" in his sights, although writing for the common man, as he noted in his brief preface. Colman's apologetic work on Genesis 1–3 had a simple premise, "If these first pages in the Book of God do not appear worthy of his Inspiration, we may eve give up the rest of the Bible."[5] Colman argued for the historicity of the book and its inspiration. "Moses certainly wrote as an historian from God."[6] Colman appealed to the content, such as the days of creation, the institution of marriage between one man and one woman, the Sabbath, and the account of the original sin, as "worthy of God."

Where did Edwards fit in? Edwards certainly lived in the shadow of Mather, but, like Colman, held fast to his Reformed Orthodox heritage. Edwards held to a six-day creation and an historical Adam.[7] But that is not to say Edwards simply held to his tradition without his typical rigorous enquiry. Edwards was indeed fascinated with the early chapters of Genesis, especially as they touched on God's creation of the world, creation of man, and the nature of man, as well as the prelapsarian covenant between Adam and God, the subsequent fall of humanity, original sin, and man's faculties in nature and grace.

This study has explored, thus far, Edwards the exegete as he used Genesis in his preaching ministry and his biblical worldview expressed in "The Redemption Discourse." Students of Edwards have long recognized the centrality of creation in his theology. Edwards's view of creation has been a topic of much interest and research. Creation is God's communication, not just his communication in terms of speech or revelation, but communication of his beauty. Creation is "an emanation of God's glory."[8] Edwards's concept of continuous creation has also gathered much attention.[9] God is continually

---

4. Colman promoted Edwards's *A Faithful Narrative*, as well as the ministry of George Whitefield.

5. Colman, *Brief Dissertation*, 2.

6. Colman, *Brief Dissertation*, 19.

7. VanDoodewaard, *Quest for the Historical Adam*, 118. That Edwards held to a literal view of Gen 1–2 is clearly indicated in his sermons on the texts of Genesis reviewed in the foregoing chapters.

8. Willem van Vlastuin, "Creation," in Stout et al., *Jonathan Edwards Encyclopedia*, 122.

9. Crisp, *Jonathan Edwards on God and Creation*; Hamilton, *Treatise on Jonathan Edwards*.

creating *ex nihilo*, which then brings into the discussion Edwards's view of God's relationship to the world. This has also been a topic of interest.[10] As Crisp points out, "unlike Aquinas, Edwards's metaphysics commits him to the notion that God has a real relation to the creation alongside a robust doctrine of divine aseity."[11] To be sure, Edwards's view is complex and grows out of his view of continuous creation and occasionalism, but nevertheless, God relates to his creation.

Edwards's view of God's goal in creation, written in one of two dissertations late in life (1755), *Concerning the End for Which God Created the World*,[12] has also attracted much interest. "The work is rightly seen as the deepest fountain of all of Edwards's theological and pastoral reflection, and is the culmination of a lifetime of reflection on the question: What is God's purpose in creating the world?"[13] God is moved to create the world because of his *ad intra* fullness, which in turn must become *ad extra*. It is no deficiency in God that moves him to create, rather it is his abundant delight in himself that moves him to create so that created beings can enter the joy and delight that God has in himself.

Edwards's view on human nature has also been well researched.[14] Edwards's treatises on *The Freedom of the Will* (1754)[15] and *Original Sin* (1758)[16] are among Edwards's most philosophical and polemical works. These works deal with human nature, or with anthropology, from Edwards's perspective, and have been given much scholarly attention over the years. Edwards would also delve into the nature of human affections, in what is probably his best-known work, *Religious Affections*.[17] Edwards's view of human nature, his anthropology, was directly related to his view of regeneration and conversion.

---

10. Crisp, "Jonathan Edwards on God's Relation to Creation," 1–16. Lee, "God's Relation to the World," 59–71.

11. Crisp, "Jonathan Edwards on God's Relation to Creation," 16.

12. *WJE* 8:401–536.

13. Joe Rigney, "The End for Which God Created the World," in Stout, *Jonathan Edwards Encyclopedia*, 196.

14. Helm, *Human Nature*; McClymond and McDermott, *Theology of Jonathan Edwards*, chs. 20–22.

15. *WJE* 1. For example, Muller, "A Careful Inquiry into the Modern Prevailing Notion of that Freedom of Will"; Helm, "Jonathan Edwards and the Absence of Free Choice" ; Muller, "Jonathan Edwards and the Parting of the Ways?"; Muller, "Jonathan Edwards and Francis Turretin on Necessity, Contingency, and Free of Will."

16. *WJE* 3. "The Great Christian Doctrine of Original Sin Defended." See Storms, *Tragedy in Eden*.

17. *WJE* 2.

But one area that seems to be neglected in Edwards's anthropology is the concept of the image of God, which finds its origin in the book of Genesis. A review of recent publications and their indices reveals a gap, which would merit a separate study. However, what follows is a sketch of Edwards's anthropology with the focus on the image of God.[18] There is only one sermon by Edwards on the key image of God text.[19] However, a search for "image of God" reveals 171 uses of "image" by Edwards.[20] Of those 171 uses, fifty-nine are a reference to Christ, the image of God, often reflecting Edwards's citation of 2 Cor 4:4, "Christ who is the image of God." The remaining 112 uses of "image of God" refer to man. Some of the references are made in passing, but there are some extended treatments on the image of God. These consistently reflect a more theological than exegetical context.

With Edwards exegetical acuity and theological precision, as well as his attention to creation and anthropology, a theology of the *imago Dei* should be discernible. This chapter will examine Edwards's understanding of man's constitution as an image-bearer. The method in this part of the study will be to selectively and chronologically analyze Edwards's interpretation of the image of God. Special attention will be given to any developments in Edwards's thinking about the image. Any study of Edwards reveals that Edwards exhibited a remarkable consistency and coherency of thought throughout his life. However, Edwards was always studying, always learning, so any development in his thinking on the image of God should also be discernible. After surveying Edwards's more significant references to the image of God, Edwards's sources will be considered and then conclusions will be made regarding his theology of the image of God.

Edwards was only eighteen years old in the summer of 1722, when he became pastor to English Presbyterian Congregation in New York City.[21] "The New York period was, by his own account, the time of Edwards's greatest religious intensity. He might subsequently have become more learned, wiser, and deeper, but he was never again to have such 'inward burnings' in his own heart."[22] One of his earliest sermons that summer in his new pastorate was from Ps 89:6, "For who in the heaven can be compared unto the LORD? Who among the songs of the mighty can be likened unto the LORD?" The doctrine was "God is infinitely exalted in gloriousness and

---

18. There is one article this student was able to find: Barone, "Relationship," 37–51.

19. Edwards, "Sermon on Gen 1:27."

20. The total search yielded 220 uses, but forty-nine were removed since they were editors' uses.

21. Edwards would pastor this congregation from August 10, 1722, to April 26, 1723. *WJE* 10:261.

22. *WJE* 10:268.

excellency above all created beings."[23] The sermon would be published as "God's Excellencies."[24] Edwards sought to set forth the "transcendent excellency" of the God who made everyone and is worshiped and adored. The sermon develops this theme of God being exalted over all his creatures in duration, greatness, excellency and loveliness, power, wisdom, holiness, and goodness. Edwards's sixth improvement is "How great must be the happiness of the enjoyment of him."[25] Edwards's language of excellency, enjoyment, and sweetness fill the application. The sixth use of the sixth improvement is eschatological, "The sweet relish of these enjoyments shall never decrease or be diminished."[26] The seventh improvement is "How excellent are they who are sanctified, and have their souls conformed unto him."[27]

It is this improvement that brings the transcendent excellency of God and the image of God together. For Edwards, it is sheer wonder and an unspeakable honor to be conformed to the image of God. This conformity to God's image is as amazing as is the ability to enjoy God. The creature is honored by being conformed to God's image in holiness. Although God is infinitely exalted above his creation in excellency and perfection, God's Spirit draws his image on those whom he sanctifies. Although Edwards does not go into the constitution of the image of God in any detail, it is clear that in God "the beauty of his beauties" is holiness and the honor of any human being is to have that holiness "drawn" upon him, being conformed to the image of God. There is an initial dignity to being created and made in the image of God, but it is even more remarkable that God should sanctify sinners and make them like himself.

The image of God in this early sermon reflects first an "excellency" in the human being. It is an honor to bear the image of God, who is the highest and most excellent and glorious being. But for Edwards, the emphasis falls upon the work of the Spirit in sanctifying the sinner, which is conforming him to God's most beautiful attribute. In this early sermon, there are strong hints of Edwards's already focusing on the restoration of the image in holiness as a major part of the image of God.

Miscellany 94 was written 1723–24. It is one of Edwards's earliest efforts at writing on the Trinity. Edwards's work on the Trinity would represent years of accumulated thinking and writing. Edwards's understanding of the Trinity is heavily influenced by his view on what it means for Christ to

23. *WJE* 10:416.
24. *WJE* 10:413–15. Master Sermon Index, 5.
25. *WJE* 10:429.
26. *WJE* 10:430.
27. *WJE* 10:430.

be the image of God. For Edwards, Christ as the image of God is not unrelated to man in the image of God, and so it is worthwhile to briefly consider this early miscellany. Edwards begins, "An absolutely perfect idea of a thing is the very thing, for it wants nothing that is in the thing, substance nor nothing else. That is the notion of the perfection of an idea, to want nothing that is in the thing."[28] God's perfect idea of himself is a substantial idea, God reflecting on himself is the begetting of his Son. God has eternally had a perfect idea of himself and so his Son is the eternally begotten Son of God, who is the image of God. God delights in his own image, and that express image whom God loves, is the Word of God.

Just as the Son is the perfect idea of God, the Spirit is the perfect act of God.

> And as to goodness, the eternal exertion of the essence of that attribute, it is nothing but infinite love, which the apostle John says is God. And as we have observed that all divine love may be resolved into God's infinite love to himself, therefore this attribute, as it was exerted from eternity, is nothing but the Holy Spirit; which is exactly agreeable to the notions some have had of the Trinity. And as to holiness, it is delight in excellency, it is God's sweet consent to himself, or in other words, his perfect delight in himself; which we have shown to be the Holy Spirit.[29]

This articulation of the persons of the Godhead is important for tracking Edwards's later development of his understanding the image of God in man. The Son is the idea of God, and the Son is the Word and wisdom of God. The Spirit is the delight God has in himself, which is the essence of his holiness. Logos and holiness mark the second and third persons of the Trinity. Although at this point Edwards makes no direct correlation to the image of God in man, it is a foundational idea that he will develop later.

"Miscellany 412" was written in 1729. That is the year that would mark the death of Solomon Stoddard and Edwards's appointment as senior pastor, as well as sickness and a physical collapse. In this miscellany, Edwards also speaks at some length on the image of God. The miscellany is on justification. Edwards is engaged in a discussion on the conditionality of salvation. In one sense, Christ fulfills the condition for salvation, but there is another sense where there are conditions on salvation which are placed on the sinner. The sinner must meet the conditions of believing in Christ, among which are universal and persevering obedience, and the fruits of love. Another condition is holiness, which means, for Edwards, to have the image of God.

---

28. *WJE* 13:258.

29. *WJE* 13:262–63.

By this Edwards does not mean the original image given at creation, rather, he means to be given the Holy Spirit, and the love of God at regeneration. "And therefore being holy is as necessary a condition of salvation as receiving money, or taking possession of goods or lands, is to becoming rich."[30] It is important to notice that for Edwards there is something about the image of God that is restored in salvation, and that is holiness, which comes from the Holy Spirit.

Shortly after "Miscellany 412," Edwards's emphasis on the image of God increases in his sermons. Edwards preached *The Pure in Heart Blessed*[31] sometime in 1730. The sermon, preached over three sermon units, is important for a couple of reasons. The first is that it demonstrates Edwards struggling to express the nature of the new birth, spiritual sight, knowledge, and experience. Edwards is working toward explaining what it means to see God. "*The Pure in Heart Blessed* clearly adumbrates Edwards's more celebrated sermon on spiritual knowledge, *A Divine and Supernatural Light*."[32] The second reason this sermon is important is there seems to be some development in Edwards's understanding of the image of God. What Edwards says about the image of God in this sermon is brief, but significant.

Edwards expounds the beatitude "blessed are the pure in heart, for they shall see God." The exposition spends considerable time on one of Edwards's favorite themes, true happiness. Edwards says the pure in heart are happy because their blessedness consists in seeing God. Then he seeks to show what is meant by seeing the invisible God. The doctrine is twofold: "[I.] It is a thing truly happifying to the soul of men to see God. [II.] The having a pure heart is the certain and only way to come to the blessedness of seeing God."[33] Since God is a spiritual being, seeing him is intellectual, "God is beheld with the understanding."[34] "But to see God is this: it is to have an immediate and certain understanding of God's excellency and love."[35] Edwards says this beholding through understanding does not come through reasoning.[36] It is in this context that Edwards speaks of the image of God.

God made man an understanding creature, man's reason is what constitutes the "natural image of God."[37] Edwards states this natural image of

---

30. *WJE* 13:472.
31. *WJE* 17:57–86. "The Pure in Heart Blessed" is the published title.
32. *WJE* 17:57.
33. *WJE* 17:61.
34. *WJE* 17:62.
35. *WJE* 7:64.
36. Edwards uses the word "ratiocination."
37. *WJE* 17:67.

God, this God-given ability to understand, is what makes him capable of intellectual delight and pleasure, which can behold and appreciate the glorious excellency and beauty of God. Edwards does not speak of a spiritual or moral image of God, and his only qualification for seeing God is that God must first make the heart pure. This involves a negative requirement, that is cleansing away the defilement of heart. Once cleansed of its filth, corruption no longer governs the heart, but is only possessed in the "inferior and exterior parts of the soul."[38] The positive element is that the soul is endowed with new qualities which enable it to delight in holy thoughts and exercises. This is the renovation of the affections and granting a new sense. What is present in this sermon is the notion that there is the natural image, which is understanding and reason. What is lacking in this sermon is a twofold division of the image as natural and spiritual, and its concomitant explanation of regeneration's effect on the image.

Edwards deals with the image of God in a sermon later from the same year, "Honey from the Rock."[39] This was a two-preaching-unit sermon. The sermon reflects a departure from Edwards's typical threefold division of exposition, doctrine, and uses. This sermon also anticipates "A Divine and Supernatural Light." Valeri notes, "He pursued the image of honey, however, in a subsequent sermon in this volume, *A Divine and Supernatural Light*. In *Honey from the Rock* Edwards uses the image to encourage praise and spiritual determination. In *A Divine and Supernatural Light*, he uses it to a remarkable effect to analyze the nature of spiritual perception, in defense of the doctrine of divine election."[40]

In "Honey from the Rock," Edwards unfolds three doctrines. "I. God causes good to arise to his elect people when they are in a state as that they are most remote from it. II. God is wont to bring good to his people out of those things that seem most unlikely to yield it. III. By causing his people to receive such great blessings from Jesus, he does, as it were, cause them to suck honey out of the rock."[41] In the second preaching unit, Edwards is applying "Christ is fitly compared to a rock."[42] Edwards then says that Christ is a rock to believers in two ways. First, he is a rock for a foundation to build upon, and second, he is a rock of defense. It is in this context that Edwards speaks with tenderness and joy of the believer who is safely at rest in Christ with the blessings of salvation. "The blessings the saints receive by Christ are

---

38. *WJE* 17:79.
39. *WJE* 17:121–39. Preached in the fall of 1730.
40. *WJE* 17:122.
41. *WJE* 17:124.
42. *WJE* 17:132.

most nourishing and perfective of their nature. The nature of man is exceedingly broken by sin in a most infirm, sickly, ruined state. The people of God do by Christ Jesus receive that grace whereby their natures are restored to a state of health and to their true excellency and perfection."[43] Here Edwards speaks of a transition in man's nature from sickness to health, from ruination to perfection. This is the restoration of man's nature in Christ. Then he states, "The Holy Spirit is given through Christ, whereby the soul is sanctified and a principle of spiritual life is infused, and the nature is renewed after the image of God."[44] Edwards again emphasizes the work of the Spirit in sanctification and the implantation of spiritual life, which is a renewal of the image of God.

The next sermon to mention image of God is "God Glorified in Man's Dependence." The sermon was delivered in Northampton in the fall of 1730 and then repreached at a clergy meeting in Boston, July 8, 1731. This sermon then appeared in print. It marks Edwards's first published work.[45] The sermon is important since it brings together a series of themes Edwards had been thinking and writing about. The small section on the image of God seems to reflect an advance in his thinking on the subject. Edwards's text is 1 Cor 1:29–31, "That no flesh should glory in his presence. But of him are ye in Christ Jesus, who of God is made unto us wisdom, and righteousness, and sanctification, and redemption: that, according as it is written, He that glorieth, let him glory in the Lord."

The doctrine is "God is glorified in the wisdom of redemption in this, that there appears in it so absolute and universal dependence of the redeemed on him."[46] In the exposition, Edwards's third point is, "The redeemed have all their good *in* God. We not only have it *of* him and *through* him, but it consists in him; he *is* all our good."[47] Edwards explains that the good of the redeemed is either objective or inherent. By objective, he means that which is outside of the redeemed which God brings to him. But the inherent good is either excellency or pleasure. "They have spiritual excellency and joy by a kind of participation of God. They are made excellent by a communication of God's excellency: God puts his own beauty, i.e., his beautiful likeness, upon their souls. They are made 'partakers of the divine

---

43. *WJE* 17:135.
44. *WJE* 17:135.
45. *WJE* 17:196.
46. *WJE* 17:202.
47. *WJE* 17:207; italics original.

nature,' or moral image of God (2 Pet 1:4)."⁴⁸ This, according to Edwards, is by the gift of the Spirit.⁴⁹

It is noteworthy that Edwards uses the term "moral image of God." Previously he spoke of the "natural image," which consists in man's understanding. Here, Edwards speak of the moral image in terms of partaking of God's nature, namely God's beauty. This is consistent with his earlier expositions regarding the restoration of the image, but here is the first noticeable time in his sermons where he speaks of a moral image, which consists of beauty, which means holiness for Edwards.

In the summer of 1731 Edwards preached the remarkably beautiful sermon, "East of Eden," which has already been analyzed. However, this sermon gives a detailed account of the original image of God at creation and then the image of God after the fall. Edwards states,

> And his soul was in a very perfect state, the faculties of it in full strength, not broken, impaired, and weakened and ruined, as they are now. The soul of man with regard to the quickness and clearness of its faculties was then like the heavenly intelligences—as a flame of fire. The natural image of God that consists in reason and understanding was then complete.
>
> And man then had excellent endowments. His mind shone with the perfect spiritual image of God, being without any defect in its holiness and righteousness, or any spot or wrinkle to mar its spiritual beauty. God had put his own beauty upon it; it shone with the communication of his glory. And man enjoyed uninterrupted spiritual peace and joy that hence arose. His mind was full of spiritual light and peace as the atmosphere in a clear and calm day.⁵⁰

Edwards uses "natural image" to denote the reason and understanding. Before the fall it was complete. Edwards also uses "spiritual image" to refer to man's original holiness and righteousness, which was his spiritual beauty. In this sermon, Edwards explains the image of God before the fall

---

48. *WJE* 17:208.

49. It appears that the renovation of the image, especially in terms of the Spirit's work of communicating God's beauty and holiness, means for Edwards some theory of theosis or deification as found in Eastern Orthodoxy. This language of participation in God, union with God, and citing 2 Pet 1:4, "partakers of the divine nature," is not rare in Edwards. However, as McClymond and McDermott point out, there is no evidence Edwards had access to the Eastern Orthodox writers (413). McClymond and McDermott demonstrate that Edwards was influenced by Neoplatonic writers, specifically the Cambridge Platonists. Although the question of Edwards's view of deification is fascinating, it is outside the scope of this research.

50. *WJE* 17:333–34.

as consisting then in two parts, the natural and the spiritual, that is understanding and the beauty of holiness. This is the first time Edwards makes this distinction in his sermons.

After the fall, the image of God is both damaged and lost. Edwards explains,

> He lost the vigor and strength of his faculties. His understanding was clouded and broken, and the whole man in all its faculties was but the ruins of what it before was. And man lost that which was his highest excellency and the proper glory of human nature, viz. his original righteousness and the spiritual image of God. And herein he lost his spiritual peace and comfort.[51]

In the application of the sermon Edwards does employ restoration language to describe salvation. There is a restoration of the happiness of the first state, and a restoration of the holiness and image of God. God's beauty is put back into fallen but redeemed people. Man's faculties are restored.

> After we have despoiled ourselves of all our primitive excellency and loveliness and become odious and in the image of Satan, we may have God's beauty put on us again; yea, we may be brought to perfect holiness as spotless as that which we lost. God is willing to restore our whole man, to exalt our faculties to a like strength and vigor with that which we had before, and our bodies to the like beauty and life.[52]

For Edwards, the understanding, that is the natural image, is still present, but severely damaged. What man lost altogether was the spiritual image. In "East of Eden" Edwards develops his dichotomous view of the image as natural and spiritual, as well as his prelapsarian and postlapsarian distinction in the image of God. Although the theme of restoration lacks symmetry, that is, Edwards does not precisely work through what components are restored and how, there is a nascent restoration theme which is unmistakable.

In August 1740 Edwards preached a two-preaching-unit sermon, "The Subjects of a First Work of Grace May Need a New Conversion."[53] Edwards's text is Luke 22:32, when Jesus says to Simon Peter, "But I have prayed for you thee, that thy faith fail not; and when thou art converted, strengthen thy brethren." Edwards's sermon is wholly pastoral, seeking to address those who were resting on an original work of grace and were not

---

51. *WJE* 17:334.
52. *WJE* 17:342.
53. *WJE* 22:183–202.

pressing on with Christ. Stout says, "Edwards's solution here is to complicate conversion."[54] Edwards tells his congregation that their faith could be easily overthrown if it were not for the prayers and strength of their mediator, Jesus Christ. Edwards then uses Peter as an example of a person who was clearly converted, and yet needed to be converted again. This may indeed have sounded like "complicating conversion," but Edwards lays out his case that "those that have true grace in their hearts may yet stand in great need of being converted."[55] Edwards shows his congregation that when a person who has received grace and has real faith, and then becomes weak in grace and faith, then another work of grace is needed which is sometimes described in terms of the first work of grace, or conversion. "When the godly are recovered and renewed after great decays and falls, this is in Scripture called by the same names as the first conversion."[56]

Edwards then summarizes the whole work of God.

> The whole work of God, from the first dawning of grace in the soul until death, may be looked upon as one work of renovation, whereby the soul is brought back from that state of sin into which we fell by the apostasy of mankind, and restoring it to its former state of holiness. It is all only a bringing back the wandering sheep by several steps. It is all only the gradual restoration of that image of God that we once had and was lost by the fall.

The destruction and death that the nature of man fell under by Adam's sin, and which it is subject to by the first birth, is restored by the second Adam in a work of grace.

> As our fall and losing of spiritual life by the first Adam was one destruction and ruin, so the renewal of it in the second Adam is by one work of restoration, which is not finished till the destruction and death that came by the first Adam is wholly removed at the conclusion of this life.[57]

Edwards's description of the work of grace as a work of renovation draws from a few themes from Genesis 1–3. First, there is restoration from the fall to the original state of holiness. This recovery is in steps and it is a gradual restoration of the image of God. The first Adam brought destruction and death, the second Adam brought grace and life as he renews what was

54. *WJE* 22:181.
55. *WJE* 22:184.
56. *WJE* 22:189.
57. *WJE* 22:190.

ruined. This work of conversion is a resurrection and a new creation. This work of conversion is putting off the old man and putting on the new man. Edwards sees conversion in terms of restoring the image of God.[58]

In another miscellany from 1741, Edwards speaks about the spiritual image of God, which is holiness. This holiness, though, is quite different from original holiness. "So gospel holiness differs greatly from the holiness of man in innocency: man had the Holy Ghost then, as the Spirit of God; but now he must have it as the Spirit of the Son of God, the Spirit of a Redeemer, a Mediator between God and us, and a spiritual husband, etc."[59] Edwards makes a direct correlation between gospel holiness, which is the restoration of the spiritual image, to the Holy Spirit as the Spirit of the Son. The restoration theme in Edwards is distinctly christocentric and requires the operations of the Holy Spirit.

From 1742–43, Edwards preached his famous sermons *Treatise Concerning Religious Affections*. Edwards's text was 1 Pet 1:8, "Whom having not seen, ye love; in whom, though now ye see him not, yet believing, ye rejoice with joy unspeakable and full of glory." The doctrine was that "true religion, in great part, consists in holy affections."[60] The sermons dealt with discerning a true work of the Spirit of God in revival. Edwards defines the affections in the first part.

> God has indued the soul with two faculties: one is that by which it is capable of perception and speculation, or by which it discerns and views and judges of things; which is called the understanding. The other faculty is that by which the soul does not merely perceive and view things, but is some way inclined with respect to the things it views or considers; either is inclined to them, or is disinclined, and averse from them; or is the faculty by which the soul doesn't behold things, as an indifferent unaffected spectator, but either as liking or disliking, pleased or displeased, approving or rejecting. This faculty is called by various names: it is sometimes called the *inclination:* and, as it has

---

58 Edwards makes similar comments in "Miscellany 847," August 1740. "Regeneration is that work of God's Spirit, whereby the soul is brought back from that state of sin into which we fell by the first apostasy of mankind, and [the Spirit] restoring it to its former state of holiness, restoring the image of God to it that was lost by the fall; but this is done gradually through the whole work of the sanctification of the Spirit. The destruction and death that the nature of man fell under by Adam, and which it is subject to by the first birth, and that new birth, in which the soul is restored by Christ, are so related one to another, that one is to be measured by the other: one consists in the removal of the other, and in restoring the soul from the other." *WJE* 20:71.

59. *WJE* 20:153.
60. *WJE* 2:95.

respect to the actions that are determined and governed by it, is called the *will*: and the *mind*, with regard to the exercises of this faculty, is often called the *heart*.[61]

Edwards's definition is partly related to the image of God. The first faculty of the soul would be the natural image, that is, the understanding. The second faculty, the inclination of the will, would be the spiritual or moral image of God, and is what is renovated in conversion by the Holy Spirit. In the third part of *Religious Affections*, Edwards points out that gracious and holy affections come through the supernatural and divine influence of the Spirit upon the heart. Gracious affections apprehend the beauty of God in his holiness. This is the restoration of the spiritual image of God.

Edwards defines the work of the Spirit also in a way that renovates both the natural image and the spiritual image. The work of the Spirit is necessary to give spiritual, supernatural understanding of divine things. Natural man, although endowed with reason and understanding due to the image of God, cannot rely on this natural understanding to understand spiritual things.

> From hence it may be surely inferred, wherein spiritual understanding consists. For if there be in the saints a kind of apprehension or perception, which is in its nature, perfectly diverse from all that natural men have, or that it is possible they should have, till they have a new nature; it must consist in their having a certain kind of ideas or sensations of mind, which are simply diverse from all that is or can be in the minds of natural men. And that is the same thing as to say, that it consists in the sensations of a new spiritual sense, which the souls of natural men have not; as is evident by what has been before, once and again observed. But I have already shown what that new spiritual sense is, which the saints have given them in regeneration, and what is the object of it. I have shown that the immediate object of it is the supreme beauty and excellency of the nature of divine things, as they are in themselves.[62]

Critical to Edwards's thesis, however, is that regeneration is not simply the ability to apprehend or understand divine things. Spiritual understanding consists of "*a sense of the heart, of the supreme beauty and sweetness of the holiness or moral perfection of divine things, together with all that discerning and knowledge of things of religion, that depends upon, and flows from such a sense.*"[63] Again, spiritual understanding and relishing, feeling, enjoying the

---

61. *WJE* 2:96.
62. *WJE* 2:271.
63. *WJE* 2:273; italics original.

excellency and beauty of God bring together both components of the image of God in Edwards.

There is also an explicit connection between the Trinity and the image of God in *Religious Affections*.

> As there are two kinds of attributes in God, according to our way of conceiving of him, his moral attributes, which are summed up in his holiness, and his natural attributes, of strength, knowledge, etc. that constitute the greatness of God; so there is a twofold image of God in man, his moral or spiritual image, which is his holiness, that is the image of God's moral excellency (which image was lost by the fall); and God's natural image, consisting in men's reason and understanding, his natural ability, and dominion over the creatures, which is the image of God's natural attributes.[64]

By 1742, Edwards is speaking of the image of God in terms of natural and spiritual image and relating it to the Trinity. Edwards continues to focus on the theme of restoration of the image in regeneration by the Holy Spirit.

The only extant sermon on the *locus classicus* is a sermon he preached in August 1751 to the Stockbridge Indians and Mohawks.[65] Edwards had arrived in Stockbridge July 1, 1751. Edwards took his post at the Indian mission after he was removed from his pastorate in Northampton. Stockbridge was both an Indian and English town. The town, however, would possess some of the same family tensions Edwards had known in Northampton, in addition to economic and political entanglements. Edwards was concerned, however, with the state of the Indians' souls. Edwards had a deep interest in the mission as missions. Marsden captures Edwards's sentiments, "For Edwards, people were not to be judged first of all by nationality, although nation was for him an important category. He did believe God dealt with nations, as the Old Testament indicated. Yet even more important was his New Testament and New Light view that distinguished the regenerate from the unregenerate within every nation."[66]

Edwards preached the gospel to the Indians and he preached it simply. Edwards's sermon on Gen 1:26–28 reflects his pastoral concerns for the souls of the Indians. "Edwards had low regard for Indian culture but high trust in Indian potential."[67] This is clearly conveyed in this sermon, which was one of his early sermons during his tenure at Stockbridge.

64. *WJE* 2:256.
65. Edwards, "Sermon on Gen 1:27."
66. Marsden, *Jonathan Edwards: A Life*, 385.
67. Marsden, *Jonathan Edwards: A Life*, 389.

Edwards's text is Gen 1:27, "So God created man in his own image, in the image of God created he him."[68] Edwards begins by stating that the image is not in the form of God's countenance or the shape of his body; God is spirit. Being made in the image of God intends two things. The first is that God gave man reason and understanding. This reflects God because he is an infinitely wise and understanding being. It is this part of the image of God in man that has the capacity to know God. It is also how man knows what is right and wrong, and what his duty toward God is. Edwards teaches the Indian congregation that creation is like a house which God prepared and furnished, and then he brought man to inhabit this grand house. Man is rule over this house and he rules with the reason and understanding given to him by God as an image-bearer.

The second part of the image of God is the most excellent part: God made man holy. Adam and Eve were "made holy, good, and upright, and without any sin and then we were made like God for God is an infinitely Holy Being."[69] Edwards then speaks of God's holiness in terms of the brightness of the sun, and the holiness in man made in his image is like holding a glass "whereby the glass shines with some image of the same brightness."[70] This second aspect of the image of God is more excellent than reason and understanding. The devil, says Edwards, has reason and understanding, but he has no holiness, therefore his reason and understanding is the worse because he has no holiness. So man, according to Edwards, consists in these two things, reason and holiness, but holiness is the more excellent of the two.

Edwards then moves to application. Edwards tells his native congregation that there is great honor in being made in the image of God, but there was a "sorrowful change" when man fell. Man "lost the image of God in as much as lost all his goodness and holiness."[71] Man did not lose his reason and understanding; that part of the image of God is retained. However, man did lose the holiness, in other words, "he lost that image of God which was most excellent and wherein man's beauty and excellency chiefly consisted."[72] When man lost the moral component of the image of God he became like the beasts. Sin so destroyed this part of the image that although man could still reason, they now have the image of the devil on their souls. Holiness is gone, wickedness has taken its place.

68. Edwards, "Sermon on Gen 1:27."
69. Edwards, "Sermon on Gen 1:27."
70. Edwards, Sermon on Gen 1:27."
71. Edwards, "Sermon on Gen 1:27."
72. Edwards, "Sermon on Gen 1:27."

The only remedy to those who now bear the image of the devil is to have Jesus Christ deliver them from their sin and "to restore the image of God in them."[73] This is an important part of Edwards's soteriology: salvation is not merely the forgiveness of sins, it is the restoration of the image of God. The restoration of the image is the restoration of holiness and happiness in the soul. The restoration of the image, being born again, is to have new hearts and be made new creatures.

Edwards then begins to apply the sermon to specific issues relevant to his native congregation. Edwards begins with the great evil of drunkenness. At first glance, this point of application may seem arbitrary on Edwards's part, but far from it. Drunkenness makes men mean and vile, which is contrary to the image of God. God had given man dignity as an image-bearer and the responsibility to rule. God made man a king to rule, but drunkenness causes a man to lose his reason and understanding. Drunkenness lowers a man's dignity as an image-bearer and makes him like a beast. Man is like a king who "wallows in the mire,"[74] like a filthy beast. In other words, drunkenness debates the natural image even more egregiously.

Edwards continues his application and says it is the image of God in man that demands that man show respect and honor to one another. Men should treat one another with civility and respect because they are all made in the image of God and that is an honorable thing. Edwards notes that Christians should especially treat one another with love and respect. Then he points out the greatness of the sin of murder, the ultimate lack of love and respect, is nothing less than destroying those made in the image of God. Edwards uses another image of God text for his support (Gen 9:6), "He that shed man's blood by man shall his blood be shed. For in the image of God made he man."[75]

The most important application, according to Edwards, is the great and glorious work of God in restoring what was spoiled and destroyed by sin. "You need therefore that God should make you over again that you may be made in the image of God again."[76] This blessed work of God is opening blind eyes and bringing men out of darkness into his marvelous light. Captives are delivered. "Hereby a hateful child of the devil is made the beautiful, lovely child of God."[77] Edwards, with vivid imagery, states, "That which is filthy like a toad or serpent, is made to shine bright with some of Christ's

---

73. Edwards, "Sermon on Gen 1:27."
74. Edwards, "Sermon on Gen 1:27."
75. Edwards, "Sermon on Gen 1:27."
76. Edwards, "Sermon on Gen 1:27."
77. Edwards, "Sermon on Gen 1:27."

beauty and brightness. That which is like a heap of dung is made on of God's precious jewels."[78] Edwards then expands on this work by stating the heart is delivered from the power of worldly affections and desires and is filled with the love of God and Christ. The mind is taken from earth and is set on heaven and heavenly things. This dimension of conversion is important because what is being done by God is a reversal of what was lost in the fall, the moral image. The final exhortation is directed to the listeners taking care that they are truly converted and "have the image of God restored to your soul by Jesus Christ."[79]

Edwards's deeply philosophical work, *A Careful and Strict Enquiry into the Modern Prevailing Notions of That Freedom of Will, Which Is Supposed to Be Essential to Moral Agency, Vertue and Vice, Reward and Punishment, Praise and Blame*,[80] was published in 1754. Edwards's work was a polemical piece against Arminianism and the self-determining views of deist Thomas Chubb, Anglican Daniel Whitby, and dissenter Isaac Watts.[81] As Edwards expounds on liberty and moral agency, he makes this comment regarding God:

> The essential qualities of a moral agent are in God, in the greatest possible perfection; such as understanding, to perceive the difference between moral good and evil; a capacity of discerning that moral worthiness and demerit, by which some things are praiseworthy, others deserving of blame and punishment; and also a capacity of choice, and choice guided by understanding, and a power of acting according to his choice or pleasure, and being capable of doing those things which are in the highest sense praiseworthy.[82]

For Edwards, God is the quintessential moral agent. God possesses perfect understanding, perfect moral perception, capacity of discernment, and capacity of choice. Then Edwards states that it is these components of God as moral agent that constitute the image of God in man. Edwards cites Gen 1:26, 26, and 9:6, and then asserts that the image of God consists of these "faculties and principles of nature." Here is why man is a moral agent. Edwards concludes, "Herein very much consists the *natural* image of God; as his *spiritual* and *moral* image, wherein man was made at first, consisted in that moral excellency, that he was endowed with."[83]

78. Edwards, "Sermon on Gen 1:27."
79. Edwards, "Sermon on Gen 1:27."
80. *WJE* 1.
81. McClymond and McDermott, *Theology of Jonathan Edwards*, 341.
82. *WJE* 1:166.
83. *WJE* 1:166.

Edwards makes a similar comment in *The End for Which God Created the World*.[84] Man is created in the image of God, which means God communicates to man the two faculties of understanding and will, or natural and spiritual image. God gives the knowledge of his glory to the understanding, and holiness, love, and joy to the will of the creature.[85]

Edwards's exegetical treatment of the image of God is found in the "Blank Bible." Trying to date the entries in the "Blank Bible" is a challenge. Edwards received the "Blank Bible" from his brother-in-law, Benjamin Pierpont, in 1730.[86] But, as Stephen Stein notes, "The 'Blank Bible' remains a chronological puzzle that has been only partially solved; Edwards wrote the entries randomly over a period of nearly three decades."[87] "The 'Blank Bible' is a chronological puzzle and an editor's nightmare."[88] Even though locating Edwards's comments on the image of God in the "Blank Bible" cannot generally be done with certainly, his observations are relevant to the overall discussion on the image of God.

First, Edwards notes that "let us make man . . . is a consultation of the persons of the Trinity about the creation of man, for every person had his particular and distinct concern in it, as well as in the redemption of man."[89] Each member of the Trinity was involved in creation and in redemption. Edwards says that the Father employed the Son and the Spirit in his work. Then Edwards comments, "The Son endued man with understanding and reason. The Holy Ghost endued him with a holy will and inclination, with original righteousness."[90] Edwards goes on, citing Plato, Ovid, and others, in exploring non-biblical accounts of the image of God in man.[91]

It is this entry in his "Blank Bible" which Edwards directly connects the persons of the Trinity with the two faculties of the image of God. "The Father employed the Son and the Holy Ghost in this work. The Son endued man

---

84. Edwards completed the first of his two dissertations, "End for Which God Created the World," in early 1755 (*WJE* 8) while in Stockbridge.

85. *WJE* 8:529.

86. *WJE* 24:1.

87. *WJE* 24:2–3.

88. *WJE* 24:104.

89. *WJE* 24:126. In a sermon on John 16:8, preached in 1729, Edwards said, "All the three persons are concerned in the salvation of man, as they were in his creation. When man was first created, there was a consultation among the persons of the Trinity. God said, 'Come and let us make man in our image, after our likeness' [Gen 1:26]." *WJE* 14:378.

90. *WJE* 24:126.

91. Edwards seems to be relying on Gale's *Court of Gentiles* for much of this information.

with understanding and reason. The Holy Ghost endued him with a holy will and inclination, with original righteousness."[92] The Son of God, the Logos, is the source of understanding and reason. The Holy Spirit, the love between the Father and the Son, is the source of holy will and original righteousness. This comports with Edwards's *Discourse on the Trinity*.[93] God's own perfect understanding or idea of himself is his image, that is, his Son. "The Scripture teaches us that Christ is the logos of God. It will appear that this logos is the same with the idea of God, whether we interpret it of the reason of God, or the word of God. If it signifies the reason or understanding of God, I suppose it won't be denied that 'tis the same thing with God's idea."[94]

The energy, love, and joy that exists between the Father and his Son is also a person, that is, the Holy Spirit.

> The Godhead being thus begotten by God's having an idea of himself and standing forth in a distinct subsistence or person in that idea, there proceeds a most pure act, and an infinitely holy and sweet energy arises between the Father and Son: for their love and joy is mutual, in mutually loving and delighting in each other. . . . The Deity becomes all act; the divine essence itself flows out and is as it were breathed forth in love and joy. So that the Godhead therein stands forth in yet another manner of subsistence, and there proceeds the third person in the Trinity, the Holy Spirit, viz. the Deity in act: for there is no other act but the act of the will.[95]

Although it is difficult to put a date on this observation, it seems that this is a later development in Edwards's thought.

A PRELIMINARY ASSESSMENT OF EDWARDS'S THEOLOGY OF THE IMAGE OF GOD AND THE REFORMED TRADITION

Edwards's theological developments and formulations were like the erection of a massive structure, with new rooms and new floors being added perennially. Edwards maintained focus and continuity of thought throughout his ministry which gave coherence to his theology, but it was not stagnant,

---

92. *WJE* 24:126.

93. *WJE* 21. Edwards worked on this on and off over many years, beginning in the early 1730s.

94. *WJE* 24:120.

95. *WJE* 24:121.

rather it grew. Norman Fiering noted, "The entire body of Jonathan Edwards's thought has a notable consistency. Ideas he sketched out in the 1720s were given full treatment thirty years later with relatively little change in substance. It is nearly futile to look for major shift or leaps, let alone retractions or reversals."[96] Edwards's view of the image of God certainly developed and grew at points, but he built on certain stable component parts.

For Edwards, the image of God was the highest part of man, it is what gave him his dignity. If God is the most excellent being in all the universe, then bearing his image gives humanity a uniqueness in the creation. Edwards saw ethical implications for the image of God. When preaching to the Stockbridge Indians, for instance, he tells them that there are sins, such as drunkenness, which make men more like beasts and degrade the dignity of God's image. The image of God requires that human beings treat each other with civility and respect. But Edwards also sees redemptive implications in the image of God, as well.

In the fall, the image was devastated. The understanding of man was clouded and corrupt, although still intact. What man lost in the image at the fall was the beauty of his original holiness. It is only in Christ that the image is restored. Edwards speaks repeatedly of conversion, or regeneration, in terms of renewal and renovation. What is renovated is the image of God. The renovation takes places when the Holy Spirit draws God's image on the sinner's soul and puts God's beauty and holiness back into his soul. The work is gradual and progressive, but nevertheless, it is a real participation and is marked by renewed affections for God and holiness.

Around 1731, Edwards begins to delineate more clearly between what he calls the natural image and the moral or spiritual image. The natural image is the reasoning, the understanding, which although tainted and clouded by sin, remains. The moral or spiritual image is holiness, love, and delight. This is what was altogether lost.

In 1742, Edwards makes an explicit connection between the image of God and persons of the Trinity. It is in the "Blank Bible" that Edwards makes another explicit connection between the Son and the Spirit and the natural and moral image. The Son, as the Logos, corresponds to man's reason and understanding. The Spirit, as love and delight, corresponds to man's holiness. The Son is analogous to the natural image. The Spirit is analogous to the spiritual image. However, the date of this entry is not exactly known.

There are two related areas that need assessment in Edwards's theology of the image of God. The first: What were Edwards's sources for understanding man's constitution as an image-bearer? Was Edwards in alignment with

---

96. Fiering, *Jonathan Edwards's Moral Thought*, 105.

the Reformed tradition on the image of God? Edwards is well-known as both traditional and innovative. Was he more innovative or traditional on the image of God? More exegetical and theological, or philosophical? The second: How did Edwards's Trinitarianism fit into his view of the image of God, or perhaps, how did Edwards's view of the image of God fit into his Trinitarianism?

When it comes to sources, the first observation that stands out is the lack of Hebrew lexical or philological data in Edwards's articulation of the image of God. Even in the "Blank Bible" where most of his exegetical and philological notes are found, Edwards makes no appeal to the key Hebrew words in Gen 1:26–27 (תּוּמְד סֶלֶצ). In a search on both "image" and "likeness," there was no data showing that Edwards appealed to the original meaning of either word. Also lacking is any appeal to the immediate context of Gen 1:26–28, for instance the function of the image in exercising dominion. There is also an absence of cross-referencing or proof-texting which could give further definition of the image of God. Although Edwards lists a series of proof texts in the "Blank Bible,"[97] it is far from clear on Edwards's thought on the relevance of these texts to the image of God. Edwards's theology of the image of God emerges without attention given to either contextual or exegetical sources.

One might think that with Edwards's fondness for Francis Turretin (1623–1687), that Turretin may be a source for him on the image of God. In a survey of Turretin on the image of God, he first denies that the image of God is participation in the divine essence. This is contrary to Edwards. Turretin then affirms three parts of the divine image, the first is the substance of the soul, that is "spiritual and incorruptible."[98] This remains after the fall. The second part is original righteousness. This is the closest parallel to Edwards, but not unique or unusual. Turretin affirms that it is this original righteousness which the first Adam lost and which the second Adam restores. The third part is both functional and ontological. There is dominion given which is part of the image (functional), and there is the immortality of the soul (ontological). With Turretin's denial of participation in the divine nature and no assertion between the natural and spiritual, or even understanding and righteousness, it appears unlikely that Turretin is Edwards's source.

---

97. Genesis 1:26. See John 1:1–4; Isa 40:13–14; Isa 9:6; 1 Cor 2:10–11; John 5:17–19; Isa 6:8; Prov 8:27–31; John 17:21–22. *WJE* 24:126. On occasion Edwards does list Eph 4:24 and Col 3:10, which are the standard NT references.

98. Turretin, *Institutes of Elenctic Theology*, 1:464–70.

In surveying Edwards's favorite theologian, Petrus van Mastricht on the image of God,[99] one quickly discovers that Mastricht is deeply exegetical and philological in dealing with Gen 1:26–29, devoting five pages to exegetical considerations. When Mastricht expounds "The Dogmatic Part," he explores what the image of God in man is. Mastricht notes that the image of God is man's conformity with God. Under this heading, Mastricht expounds on the faculties of the soul. Mastricht of course asserts original righteousness, immortality, and the functional quality of dominion, but most interestingly, he states in section 32 that the faculties of the soul, which bear the divine image, are the intellect, will, and affections. These faculties reflect what is in God himself. Significantly, Mastricht also notes that a variety of the faculties appears to "adumbrate" the plurality of persons of the Godhead, who are one in essence.

First, this comports with Edwards's view that the image is intellect, will, and affections. What merits attention is that although Edwards delineates between natural and moral image, and Mastricht does not, all the component parts (intellect, will, and affections) are present in Mastricht's description. Second, although Edwards does indeed conclude that the faculties reflect the second and third members of the Holy Trinity, Mastricht acknowledges that some level of correspondence between man's faculties and the members of the Godhead is "adumbrated."

Edwards, in his Catalogue of Books, listed John Glas, *Some Notes on Scripture-Texts, Shewing the Import of These Names of Jesus Christ, the Son of God and the Word of God, with an Account of the Image of God in Man* (London, 1748).[100] This appears to be the only book with an emphasis on the image of God. Glas (1695–1773) was the father-in-law of Robert Sandeman, and an advocate of the Glasite church, later Sandemandianism.[101] In examining Glas's work, there is really nothing significant about his work on the image of God that is reflected in Edwards. Glas uses the category of "sensitive life,"[102] to describe what distinguished Adam from plants and beasts. It was this sensitive life, according to Glas, that was engaged in the first transgression and lost in the first transgression. Glas affirms that Christ is the only perfect image of God. Glas uses "new creation" to describe the restoration, which he sees as eschatological. Although Edwards cites Glas numerous times, he never does so in relation to the image of God.

---

99. Mastricht, *Theoretico-Practica Theologia*, 378–88.
100. *WJEO* 26:319.
101. *WJEO* 26:45.
102. Glas, *Some Notes on Scripture-Texts*, 29.

Edwards's ministerial friend and correspondent, Benjamin Colman, had written a sequel to his *A Brief Dissertation on the Three First Chapters of Genesis* (1735). Colman's 1736 work was *A Dissertation in the Image of God Wherein Man Was Created*. Although Colman's book is not in Edwards's catalogue, he must have been aware of it. Colman's work, unlike Glas's, has some similarities with Edwards. The first notable observation is that Colman quotes van Mastricht on his title page, and then later cites him. "Under this Head I will insert the learned and pious Peter van Mastricht his reasons of God's making Man in his own Image."[103] Colman asserts that "God made Man in his own Image in respect of Intellect and Understanding, Knowledge and Wisdom."[104] Colman also emphasized that "man was eminently created by God in his own image, after his likeness, in respect of sanctity and holiness, integrity and rectitude. There is a moral as well as intellectual perfection."[105] Although Colman does not distinguish the categories as Edwards does, natural and moral, they certainly are present in Colman's exposition of the image. Furthermore, while Colman does not correlate these faculties to the Trinity, he certainly sees these faculties as the "Stamp and Impress of God."[106] Although Edwards does not cite Colman's work, nor is there evidence of him owning or borrowing the book,[107] there are distinct similarities.

Edwards's view that the image of God is that which makes man unique and gives him dignity is commonplace in theology. Edwards's teaching that original righteousness in the image is also commonplace. Original righteousness as part of the image is taught by Turretin and Mastricht, as well as Matthew Poole and Matthew Henry. Matthew Poole has commented on Gen 1:26 that the third part of the image is "in the singular endowments wherewith God hath adorned it, as *knowledge, righteousness,* and *true holiness*, in which St. Paul chiefly placeth this image, Eph. iv. 24; Col. iii.10."[108] Matthew Henry's comments are similar, also in the third part of the image, "In his purity and rectitude. God's image upon man consists in knowledge, righteousness and true holiness, Eph. iv. 24 Col. iii.10."[109]

---

103. Colman, *Dissertation on the Image of God*, 27.
104. Colman, *Dissertation on the Image of God*, 8.
105. Colman, *Dissertation on the Image of God*, 11.
106. Colman, *Dissertation on the Image of God*, 15.
107. A search on Benjamin Colman yields 152 occurrences, none of which reference his book on the image of God.
108. Poole, *Annotations*, 1:4; italics original.
109. Henry, *Exposition*, 1:10.

These themes found in Edwards are shared within Edwards's theological and commentarial tradition. However, what about his view of a distinction between natural image, consisting of understanding and reason, and spiritual understanding, consisting of holiness? Although there is nothing like this in Turretin, Mastricht, Poole, and Henry comment on the nature of the soul in a similar way. Poole comments, for instance, the image consists "in its powers and faculties, reason or understanding, and freedom in its choices and actions."[110] Henry stated, "The soul of man, considered in its three noble faculties, understanding, will, and active power, is perhaps the brightest clearest looking-glass in nature, wherein to see God."[111] Although there are clear connections between Mastricht, Poole, Henry, and Edwards in that image consists of holiness, understanding, and will, Edwards makes a fundamental distinction not found in his favorite commentators or theologians; that is, the reason or understanding is the natural image and holiness is the spiritual image.

At this point, it seems that this is an area of Edwards's theology where he is also drawing from his philosophical perspective. Even though Edwards was in a tradition that "had been attempting to abolish moral philosophy,"[112] Edwards did not seek to abolish it, but rather to integrate and use it. In the words of Norman Fiering, "Edwards, on the contrary, tried to have it both ways."[113] There is no doubt that Edwards embraced integration of philosophy and theology, but certainly within a framework of his Reformed and Puritan theological tradition. This is an important observation when it comes to Edwards's theology of the image of God. Although theological and exegetical sources for elements of his view are present, the nuanced definitions and distinctions are not. It seems here that one needs to consider Edwards's moral philosophy as well.

For Edwards, the natural image was identified with understanding and reason, but "according to Edwards, the most important function of natural understanding or intellect in the moral life is the exercise of conscience."[114] In Edwards's view, the image of God both in the "regenerate and unregenerate alike, sinners and saints, have the common faculties of understanding, will, and sentience."[115] An unconverted person has understanding as well as

---

110. Poole, *Annotations*, 1:4.
111. Henry, *Exposition*, 1:10.
112. Fiering, *Jonathan Edwards's Moral Thought*, 49.
113. Fiering, *Jonathan Edwards's Moral Thought*, 49.
114. Fiering, *Jonathan Edwards's Moral Thought*, 62.
115. Fiering, *Jonathan Edwards's Moral Thought*, 65.

conscience. He has an awareness of the guilt of sin and even the judgment of God, but he has not a disposition or inclination toward God.

Edwards said in "Miscellany 732," around 1738,

> The judgment is capable of being convinced of evil. Men's natural reason is capable of discerning force in those arguments that prove it. Though sin greatly clouds the judgment concerning these things, a natural man's reason, by common assistance of it against the clouding, prejudicing and stupefying nature of sin, is capable of seeing the force of many arguments that prove God's anger and future punishment, and the greatness of these things. And so a natural man is capable of being convinced how much there is in him contrary to God's law, and to how great a degree it is contrary, and what connection there is between these faults and God's anger and future punishment.[116]
>
> The mind of the natural man has "speculative" or "notional" understanding, but he altogether lacks a sense of delight in God or relish in holiness. Edwards noted in the same Miscellany, he is capable of a deeply impressed, and lively and affecting idea and sense of these things, which is something more than a mere conviction in the judgment concerning their truth. The mind of a natural man is capable of a sense of the heart of natural [evil], or of those things that are terrible to nature.[117]

The source for this view of human faculties, says Fiering, is Edwards's metaphysics.

It is important to note that Fiering does not relate understanding or other faculties to the image of God, only to Edwards's anthropology in general. However, Fiering's explanation of Edwards's position comports with all that has been demonstrated regarding Edwards's view of the divine image. Fiering carefully traces the sources in Edwards's thinking on understanding to Samuel Clarke. "Edwards was profoundly indebted, I believe, to Samuel Clarke above all for providing him with an up-to-date intellectualist theory of ethics that accounted for the moral understanding of the natural man. After Edwards read Clarke there is a detectable shift in his thinking."[118]

For Edwards, there was a "rational structure" to the universe. This would correspond to Edwards's view of Christ as the Logos. That rational structure is reflected in the natural understanding or reason that is in man, which is Edwards's view of the natural image. However, man is not complete,

---

116. *WJE* 18:358.
117. *WJE* 18:358.
118. Fiering, *Jonathan Edwards's Moral Thought*, 87.

let alone redeemed, by the understanding or reason alone. Something else must happen in him beyond what is in him by nature, and that is a "new sense of the heart" or, as has been demonstrated, the renewal of the moral image. It must be noted that for Edwards, the Spirit also renews the understanding (the natural image) by giving new apprehensions of the gospel and new sight of its beauty. This is a point that is easily lost, but Edwards was clear:

> Now, it is evident from the Scripture that this knowledge of divine things which the true saints have is what others have nothing of. *1 Corinthians 2:14*, "The natural man receiveth not." *1 John 3:6*, "Whosoever sinneth hath not seen him nor known him." *3 John 11*, "He that doeth evil hath not seen God." The meaning can't be that he has not a doctrinal knowledge [of God, or] acquaintance with the doctrines [of the gospel]. This knowledge consists in the mind's apprehension and view of the moral excellency and glory of the objects of faith, as is evident [in] *2 Corinthians 4:3–4*, "But if our gospel be hid, it is hid to them that are lost: in whom the god of this world hath blinded the minds of them which believe not, lest the light of the glorious gospel of Christ, who is the image of God, should shine unto them." [Also in] *2 Corinthians 4:6*, "For God, who commanded the light to shine out of darkness, hath shined in our hearts, to give the light of the knowledge of the glory of God in the face of Jesus Christ." [And] with [the] foregoing chapter, *2 Corinthians 4:18*, "But we all, with open face beholding as in a glass the glory of the Lord, are changed into the same image from glory to glory, even as by the Spirit of the Lord." It is the moral excellency [of divine things], because the image [of Jesus Christ in the light of the gospel] is the moral image [of God]. This knowledge, you see, sinners [cannot have]. They that live in sin are spoken of as wholly destitute of [it], and therefore it is different in kind from all that doctrinal knowledge they have. And this being implied in saving faith, and being fundamental in it, this is the first thing wherein the essential difference lies between [saving and common faith].[119]

But the major work of renovation is in new affections, that is, dispositions and inclinations of the will, and this is nothing less than the restoration of the moral image which was lost at the fall. An unregenerate person may understand the rational truths of God, judgment, the gospel, but he has no relish in them. The Holy Spirit renovates the will, that is, the inclinations

---

119. *WJEO* 25:510.

and affections of the heart. This is altogether supernatural. This fits within Edwards's larger metaphysical views of nature and grace.

Fiering points out that Edwards was "deeply influenced, I believe, by Samuel Clarke's formulations and before that by Malebranche's."[120] However, as Fiering notes, Edwards moves beyond the "rational foundations of ethics," and as a supernaturalist, in the Reformed tradition, asserts that "for the whole man to be ethical—in will, or affections, as well as in understanding—nature is not enough."[121]

The next area of assessment is the way Edwards related the image of God to the Trinity. Edwards, as noted, specifically connected the Trinity to the image of God of man in *Religious Affections* and in the "Blank Bible." Recently, Marco Barone has written, "It seems safe to identify the moral attributes with the Holy Spirit, who is also the will of God, and the natural attribute, who is the understanding of God."[122] Barone deals with some apparent tensions in Edwards's construction, but his main concern is to see how Edwards's view of the nature of God shapes his anthropology. "In light of Edwards's view of the God's natural image in mankind, it seems reasonable to suppose that the New Englander draws this conclusion because of his doctrine of God's natural image in humanity, according to which he formal structure of mankind's and God's faculties are structurally the same when it comes to respective possession of understanding and will."[123]

The correspondence between Edwards's Trinitarianism and the image of God is clear, but it seems not have fully developed until the early 1740s. Edwards's corresponding categories, however, do overlap some when it comes to redemption. As noted above, the understanding needs to be illuminated by the Holy Spirit. The recreation of the moral or spiritual image, which corresponds to the Spirit, is a recreation in the image of the Second Adam. So although Edwards's categories were nuanced in terms of the persons of the Trinity, he never allowed his metaphysics to override the clear redemptive roles of the Son and the Spirit.

In summary, the image of God was a crucial piece in Edwards's anthropology and soteriology. Even though Edwards's anthropology has received much scholarly attention, not much has focused on the image of God. Edwards's source for his theology of the image of God was roughly framed by his Reformed tradition, represented by Mastricht, Poole, and Henry, but

---

120. Fiering, *Jonathan Edwards's Moral Thought*, 93. Nicolas Malebranche (1638–1715) was a French Jesuit, and a Cartesian philosopher.

121. Fiering, *Jonathan Edwards's Moral Thought*, 104.

122. Barone, "Relationship between God's Nature," 40.

123. Barone, "Relationship between God's Nature," 42.

was refined by his moral philosophy, shaped primarily by Clarke and Malebranche. Although Edwards's philosophical perspectives are present, this study is critically appreciative, observing that Edwards was in fact committed to the supremacy of Scripture and the Reformed theological tradition, so his philosophical emphasis on "understanding" alone could not account for the totality of image of God or the work of regeneration. Edwards complements his exegetical and theological perspective on the image of God with his metaphysical perspective, which provided Edwards with a more nuanced view of the divine image in his anthropology. Edwards's Trinitarianism also significantly shaped his view of the image of God over the course of his ministry. Edwards's view of the divine image in many ways reflects the complexity and integrationist tendencies in Edwards's thought.

Conclusion and Prospect

EDWARDS ON GENESIS

"Yet the oversight of the importance of the Bible to Edwards has kept us from the true Jonathan Edwards."[1] Thus said Stephen Nichols. This study has used the book of Genesis as a window to contribute to "the true Jonathan Edwards." This view through Genesis has revealed Edwards's hermeneutical and homiletical approaches. Stephen Nichols, in his important work, has shown that Edwards typology "comprised a single coherent system."[2] The typological meaning of Scripture is spiritual, and requires the Holy Spirit to give insight. Edwards never minimized the historical, but the typological required a "new sense." This view of Edwards as a typologist was certainly seen in his treatment of Genesis. But the Genesis sermons also showed that Edwards was not always consumed with typology or giving the "spiritual sense." At times his typology was abundant (e.g., sermon 381, on Gen 28:12, Jacob at Bethel). At other times his typology was greatly restrained (e.g., sermon 464, on Gen 39:12, Joseph fleeing temptation). And at other times his typology was completely absent (sermon 434, on Gen 12:2, Abraham being blessed and a blessing). Edwards's use of Genesis demonstrates his typological exegesis, but it also shows a priority on pastoral, applicatory, and ethical preaching. In other words, his typology did not always serve the sermon as it was preached to his congregation. As such this study has sought to contribute to Edwards scholarship in the following ways.

1. Nichols, *Jonathan Edwards's Bible*, 1.
2. Nichols, *Jonathan Edwards's Bible*, 13.

Barshinger's work took one book of the Bible, the Psalms, to explore Edwards the exegete.³ Edwards used the book of Psalms extensively, quoting it more than any other book of the Bible. Barshinger clearly showed that Edwards's theological engagement with the Psalms colored his life and ministry. Barshinger describes Edwards's use of the Psalms as "redemptive-historical." Barshinger correctly sees Edwards as committed to the Protestant and Puritan tradition of both historical and typological exegesis, keeping him within his pre-critical exegetical world. Barshinger sees a big picture in Edwards's exegesis of the Psalms, and that is a redemptive-historical framework where he uses christological and ecclesiological typology in interpreting and applying the Psalms. This redemptive-historical emphasis is also and certainly present in Edwards's use of Genesis, as shown in this study. Edwards sees Christ in the book of Genesis; he sees the believer and unbeliever typified in the lives of Cain, Jacob, and Joseph. Barshinger's work, moreover, brings out Edwards's Christ-centered gospel preaching to the life of the church, as reflected in the Psalms. One of Barshinger's observations on Edwards on the Psalms, then, finds a strong correlation in his use of Genesis, as shown in chapter 3 and 4 of this study, echoing that "Edwards interpreted . . . devotionally, reading the book in straightforward literal ways that related to Christian piety and holiness."⁴

Sweeney's work⁵ has a broader scope than either Nichols, Barshinger, or this study. But Sweeney's observations about Edwards's view of the Bible, his view of preaching, and his eclecticism as an exegete can be extended to Edwards's use of Genesis. Sweeney's point that Edwards did things with the Bible that most scholars and pastors would not do today is being challenged with a resurgence of pre-critical and theological exegesis, but the point is still well-taken. Sweeney's view that Edwards comes to the Scripture from a multitude of exegetical and theological angles was certainly demonstrated in his use of Genesis, as shown in chapters 3 and 4, the sermons on Genesis in the periods 1727–1735 and 1736–1739, and the "Redemption Discourse" (ch. 5). However, an area that Sweeney only briefly touched on deserves much more attention as one considers Edwards's use of Genesis; that is, practical knowledge or "the doctrine of living to God by Christ."⁶ This aspect of Edwards's exegesis and exposition as the driving force behind his applicatory, ethical, exemplary preaching is demonstrated more in this study than Sweeney's cursory treatment indicated.

3. Barshinger, *Jonathan Edwards and the Psalms*, 2014.
4. Barshinger, *Jonathan Edwards and the Psalms*, 273.
5. Sweeney, *Edwards the Exegete*.
6. Sweeney, *Edwards the Exegete*, 197.

Furthermore, Edwards's exemplary preaching is the missing theme in each of these treatments. Barshinger comes closest to recognizing it, but lacks the specificity this study has sought to demonstrate. For Edwards there was no tension between preaching Christ within the framework of redemptive history and using OT figures as moral examples. Edwards was just as much at home uncovering the typological meaning of the stone at Bethel as he was turning Cain or Abraham into a moral model to be shunned or followed. Scholarly analysis of Edwards cannot neglect his intensely pastoral preaching. Sometimes, as has been observed in this study, this pastoral impulse in Edwards was so strong that he bypassed obvious typological issues for the sake of staying on target in driving home the truth to the consciences of his auditors. Although many would call some of his sermons moralistic, Edwards's exemplary preaching usually remained within the context of the gospel. Furthermore, the exemplary and applicatory emphasis revealed his pastoral heart for his congregation.

EDWARDS ON THE IMAGE OF GOD

Although Edwards has only one Genesis sermon on the image of God,[7] the image of God was a profoundly significant topic in Edwards's anthropology, and the lack of attention in scholarship is surprising. Edwards was theologically innovative and internally consistent, as well as demonstrably progressive, in his articulation of the image of God. This is often a missing piece in studies on Edwards's anthropology, but it is a major emphasis in both his understanding of man's dignity, man's faculties, man's depravity, man's redemption, and his constitutional correlation to the Trinity.

Edwards's theology of the image certainly saw some developments and refinements, but he stayed within his substantive Trinitarian framework. This should be no surprise. "His trinitarianism ran like a subterranean river throughout his career as a pastor and polemicist," said Amy Plantinga Pauw.[8] Edwards's sources for his understanding of the image of God seem to be both his theological and exegetical tradition and then honed or sharpened by his own moral philosophy. On the one hand, there are traces of Mastricht, Poole, Henry, and possibly Colman, in his theological formulation of the image. On the other hand, there are traces of his moral philosophy. Edwards's integration of theology and philosophy are manifest in his view of the image of God. Edwards on the image of God reflects his creativity, his theological genius and consistency, his philosophical acumen, as well as his

---

7. Sermon 998. Gen 1:27, Aug. 1751.
8. Pauw, *Supreme Harmony of All*, 3.

commitment to continuing to think and reflect on a subject over the years. Clearly, more research needs to be done this area, as it deserves a dedicated study of Edwards's anthropology—but a sketch is provided in the context of research on Edwards's use of the book of Genesis.

PROSPECT

The work of the Jonathan Edwards Center at Yale University has opened new horizons and capabilities in Edwards research through the digital editions, ongoing research, and publications. There are numerous areas that need further investigation. First, the sermon index allows research on Edwards's sermons to be conducted both canonically and chronologically. This study has demonstrated through Edwards's use of Genesis that Edwards the exegete cannot be isolated from Edwards the preaching pastor. Edwards's handling of various books of the Bible, most of which is unmined at this point, can continue the trajectory of filling out the picture of Edwards and his Bible. A chronological study could open new perspectives on how Edwards grew as a homiletician and an exegete. Second, the embarrassment of riches in Edwards's "Blank Bible," "Notes on Scripture," and "Miscellanies" offer more in terms of Edwards's exegetical method and theological formulation. Tracing out neglected areas of his theology, his sources, and the connections to his overall system still demands attention. Edwards on the Trinity or justification or the atonement or eschatology has garnered much attention for legitimate reasons. But what about other areas that have not been explored? For instance, in terms of contemporary concerns, did Edwards have a theology of gender? Did Edwards have a detailed theology of the conscience or work or natural law?

More investigation is warranted on the trajectory of Edwards as man between two worlds: the pre-critical world of Mastricht, Turretin, Poole, Henry, and Doddridge, and his Enlightenment world of Locke, Clarke, and Malebranche. Did the heirs of Edwards follow the man from the pre-critical world or the Enlightenment world? Did they follow his hermeneutics? Did Hopkins and Bellamy continue his view of Bible interpretation? Is Edwards even reproducible? With the resurgence of traditional exegesis, can Edwards contribute to the enterprise today? It seems so.

Bibliography

PRIMARY SOURCES

Colman, Benjamin. *A Brief Dissertation of the Three First Chapters of Genesis. Giving Some of the Evident Signatures of the Inspiration of God in those First Pages of Holy Oracles*. Boston, 1735.

———. *A Dissertation on the Image of God Wherein Man Was Created*. Boston, 1736.

Edwards, Jonathan. *The Blessing of God: Previously Unpublished Sermons of Jonathan Edwards*. Edited by Michael D. McMullen. Nashville: Broadman & Holman, 2003.

———. *Sermons by Jonathan Edwards on the Matthean Parables*. 3 vols. Edited by Kenneth P. Minkema et al. New Haven: The Jonathan Edwards Center at Yale University, 2012.

———. *The Sermons of Jonathan Edwards: A Reader*. Edited by Wilson H. Kimnach et al. New Haven: Yale University Press, 1999.

———. *The Works of Jonathan Edwards, A.M.* London, 1834.

———. *The Works of Jonathan Edwards*. 26 vols. New Haven: Yale University Press, 1957–2019.

———. *The Works of Jonathan Edwards Online*. 46 vols. New Haven: The Jonathan Edwards Center at Yale University, 2008. http://edwards.yale.edu/archive/.

Glas, John. *Some Notes on Scripture-Texts, Shewing the Import of These Names of Jesus Christ, the Son of God and the Word of God, with an Account of the Image of God in Man*. London, 1748.

Henry, Matthew. *Exposition of the Old and New Testaments*. 6 vols. London, 1708–1710.

Hopkins, Samuel. *The Life and Character of the Late Reverend Jonathan Edwards*. Boston, 1765. PRDL.

Mastricht, Petrus van. *Theoretico-practica theologia*. Utrecht, 1698.

Poole, Matthew. *Annotations upon the Holy Bible*. 3 vols. London, 1700.

———. *Synopsis criticorum aliorumque Sacræ Scripturæ interpretum*. London, 1669–1676.

Turretin, Francis. *Institutes of Elenctic Theology*. Translated by George Musgrave Giger. Edited by James T. Dennison Jr. Philipsburg, NJ: Presbyterian and Reformed, 1992.

———. *Institutio Theologiae Elencticae*. Geneva, 1680–1683.

SECONDARY SOURCES

Abernathy, Andrew T. "Jonathan Edwards as Multi-dimension Bible Interpreter: A Case Study from Isaiah 40–55." *Journal of the Evangelical Theological Society* 56 (2013) 815–30.

Barone, Marco. "The Relationship between God's Nature, God's Image in Man, and Freedom in the Philosophy of Jonathan Edwards." *Jonathan Edwards Studies* 8 (2018) 37–51.

Barshinger, David P. *Jonathan Edwards and the Psalms: A Redemptive-Historical Vision of Scripture*. Oxford: Oxford University Press, 2014.

Barshinger, David P., and Douglas A. Sweeney, eds. *Jonathan Edwards and Scripture: Biblical Exegesis in British North America*. Oxford: Oxford University Press, 2018.

Bogue, Carl W. *Jonathan Edwards and the Covenant of Grace*. Eugene, OR: Wipf and Stock, 2008.

Brown, Robert E. *Jonathan Edwards and the Bible*. Bloomington: Indiana University Press, 2002.

Calhoun, Robert L. "The Role of Historical Theology." *Journal of Religion* 21 (1941) 444–54.

Chapman, Alister, et al., eds. *Seeing Things Their Way: Intellectual History and the Return of Religion*. Notre Dame: Notre Dame University Press, 2009.

Crisp, Oliver D. *Jonathan Edwards on God and Creation*. Oxford: Oxford University Press, 2012.

———. "Jonathan Edwards on God's Relation to Creation." *Jonathan Edwards Studies* 8 (2018) 1–16.

Fiering, Norman. *Jonathan Edwards's Moral Thought and Its British Context*. Chapel Hill: University of North Carolina Press, 1981.

Finn, Nathan A., and Jeremy M. Kimble, eds. *A Reader's Guide to the Major Writings of Jonathan Edwards*. Wheaton, IL: Crossway 2017.

Hamilton, S. Mark. *A Treatise on Jonathan Edwards: Continuous Creation and Christology*. N.p.: JESociety, 2017.

Helm, Paul. *Human Nature from Calvin to Edwards*. Grand Rapids: Reformation Heritage, 2018.

———. "Jonathan Edwards and the Parting of the Ways?" *Jonathan Edwards Studies* 4 (2014) 42–60.

Kreider, Glenn R. *Jonathan Edwards' Interpretation of Revelation 4:1—8:1*. Dallas: University of America Press, 2004.

Lee, Sang Hyune, ed. *The Princeton Companion to Jonathan Edwards*. Princeton: Princeton University Press, 2005.

Lesser, M. X. *Reading Jonathan Edwards: An Annotated Bibliography in Three Parts, 1729–2005*. Grand Rapids: Eerdmans, 2007.

Lovi, David S., and Benjamin Westerhoff. *The Power of God: A Jonathan Edwards Commentary on the Book of Romans*. Eugene, OR: Pickwick, 2013.

Marsden, George M. *Jonathan Edwards: A Life*. New Haven: Yale University, 2003.

McClymond, Michael J., and Gerald R. McDermott. *The Theology of Jonathan Edwards.* Oxford: Oxford University Press, 2012.

Minkema, Kenneth P. "A Chronology of Edwards' Life and Writings." New Haven: Jonathan Edwards Center at Yale University. http://edwards.yale.edu/research/chronology.

———. "Jonathan Edwards in the Twentieth Century." *Journal of the Evangelical Theological Society* 47 (2004) 659–87.

———. "Old Age and Religion in the Writings and Life of Jonathan Edwards." *Church History* 70 (2001) 674–704.

Muller, Richard A. "Jonathan Edwards and Francis Turretin on Necessity, Contingency, and Free of Will. In Response to Paul Helm." *Jonathan Edwards Studies* 4 (2014) 266–85.

———. "Jonathan Edwards and the Absence of Free Choice: A Parting of Ways in the Reformed Transition." *Jonathan Edwards Studies* 1 (2011) 3–22.

———. *Post-Reformation Reformed Dogmatics: The Rise and Development of Reformed Orthodoxy, ca. 1520 to ca. 1725.* Grand Rapids: Baker Academic, 2003.

Muller, Richard A., and John L. Thompson, eds. *Biblical Interpretation in the Era of the Reformation.* Grand Rapids: Eerdmans, 1996.

Murray, Iain. *Jonathan Edwards: A New Biography.* Edinburgh: Banner of Truth, 1987.

Neele, Adriaan C. *Before Jonathan Edwards: Sources of New England Theology.* Oxford: Oxford University Press, 2019.

Nichols, Stephen R. C. *Jonathan Edwards' Bible: The Relationship of the Old and New Testaments.* Eugene, OR: Pickwick, 2013.

Noll, Mark A. "Jonathan Edwards' Use of the Bible: A Case Study (Genesis 32:22–32) with Comparisons." *Jonathan Edwards Studies* 2 (2012) 30–46.

Pauw, Amy Plantinga. *The Supreme Harmony of All: The Trinitarian Theology of Jonathan Edwards.* Grand Rapids: Eerdmans, 2002.

Schafer, Thomas A., and Adriaan C. Neele, eds. "A Chronological List of Jonathan Edwards' Sermons and Discourses." New Haven: Jonathan Edwards Center at Yale University, 2007.

Stein, Stephen J., ed. *The Cambridge Companion to Jonathan Edwards.* New York: Cambridge, 2007.

———. "Cotton Mather and Jonathan Edwards on the Epistle of James: A Comparative Study." In *Cotton Mather and the Biblia Americana, America's First Bible Commentary: Essays in Reappraisal,* edited by Reiner Smolinski and Jan Stievermann, 363–82. Tubingen: Mohr Siebeck, 2010.

———. "'Like Apples of Gold in Pictures of Silver': The Portrait of Wisdom in Jonathan Edwards' Commentary on the Book of Proverbs." *Church History* 54 (1985) 324–37.

Steinmetz, David C. "The Superiority of Pre-Critical Exegesis." *Theology Today* 37 (1980) 27–38.

Storms, Samuel C. *Tragedy in Eden: Original Sin in the Theology of Jonathan Edwards.* Lanham, MD: University of America Press, 1985.

Stout, Harry S., et al., eds. *The Jonathan Edwards Encyclopedia.* Grand Rapids: Eerdmans, 2017.

Sweeney, Douglas A. *Edwards the Exegete: Biblical Interpretation and Anglo-Protestant Culture on the Edge of the Enlightenment.* Oxford: Oxford University Press, 2016.

———. *Jonathan Edwards and the Ministry of the Word: A Model of Faith and Thought*. Downers Grove: InterVarsity, 2009.

Tracy, Patricia J. *Jonathan Edwards, Pastor: Religion and Society in Eighteenth-Century Northampton*. New York: Hill and Wang, 1980.

Westra, Helen. *The Minister's Task and Calling in the Sermons of Jonathan Edwards*. Lewiston, NY: Mellen, 1986.

VanDoodewaard, William. *The Quest for the Historical Adam: Genesis, Hermeneutics, and Human Origins*. Grand Rapids: Reformation Heritage, 2015.

Yoo, Jeongmo. "Jonathan Edwards' Interpretation of the Major Prophets." *Puritan Reformed Journal* 3 (2011) 160–92.

Name Index

Abernathy, Andrew, 13
Aquinas, Thomas, 81

Barone, Marco, 82, 106
Barshinger, David, 3–7, 12–14, 75–76, 109–10
Bedford, Arthur, 68
Bogue, Carl, 67
Brainerd, David, 2, 21, 40
Brown, Robert, 17
Buxtorf, Johann, 21

Calhoun, Robert, 15
Chapman, Alister, 4
Chubb, Thomas, 96
Clarke, Samuel, 104, 106–7, 111
Colman, Benjamin, 80, 102, 110
Crisp, Oliver, 80–81

Doddridge, Philip, 18, 21–22, 111
Dwight, Timothy, 21

Edwards Jr., Jonathan, 65
Edwards, John, 25
Edwards, Jonathan
  "Apocalyptic Writings", 23, 40
  "Blank Bible", 5, 7, 11, 13–14, 21–22, 43, 68, 71–74, 97, 99–100, 106, 111

A Careful and Strict Enquiry into the Modern Prevailing Notions of That Freedom of Will, 96
Concerning the End for Which God Created the World, 81, 96–97
Diary, 3
Discourse on the Trinity, 97–98
Ethical Writings, 11
A Faithful Narrative, 46, 63, 80
The Freedom of the Will, 14, 81
  "The Harmony of the Old and New Testament", 11
A History of the Work of Redemption, 14, 40, 56, 64–75
  "The Life of David Brainerd", 40
  "Miscellanies", 11, 29, 56, 71, 73, 83–85, 91, 104, 111
  "Notes on Scripture", 5, 7, 11, 14, 40, 111
Original Sin, 30, 81
  "Redemption Discourse", 16, 63–75, 80, 109
  "Resolutions", 3
A Treatise Concerning Religious Affections, 11, 81, 91–93, 106
  "Typological Writings", 14, 40
Edwards, Timothy, 21, 25–26
Erskine, John, 65

Fiering, Norman, 99, 103–4, 106

Name Index

Finn, Nathan, 2

Gerstner, John, 10
Glas, John, 101
Gregory, Brad, 4

Hall, Richard, 19
Hamilton, S. Mark, 80
Helm, Paul, 81
Henry, Matthew, 18, 21, 33, 36, 38–39, 71, 102–3, 106, 110–11
Hopkins, Samuel, 22, 50, 111

Kimble, Jeremy, 2
Kimnach, Wilson, 25–26
Kreider, Glenn, 13

Lee, Sang Hyune, 81
Lesser, M. X., 1
Locke, John, 19, 111
Lovi, David, 10–11

Malebranche, Nicolas, 106–7, 111
Marsden, George, 2–3, 27, 33, 42, 46, 51, 93
Mastricht, Petrus van, 10, 26, 67, 101–3, 106, 110–11
Mather, Cotton, 25, 79–80
McClymond, Michael, 65–66, 88, 96
McDermott, Gerald, 65–66, 88, 96
Miller, Perry, 2, 10
Minknema, Kenneth, 2, 29, 38
Muller, Richard, 18, 81
Murray, Iain, 2

Neele, Adriaan, 19, 21–22, 27, 29, 33, 38, 42, 46, 50
Newton, Isaac, 19
Nichols, Stephen, 4, 11–12, 75–76, 108
Noll, Mark, 35

Pauw, Amy Plantinga, 110
Perkins, William, 26
Pierpont, Benjamin, 14, 97
Poole, Matthew, 18, 21–22, 36, 62, 71, 102–3, 106, 110–11

Rigney, Joe, 81

Sandeman, Robert, 101
Schafer, Thomas, 27, 29, 33, 38, 42, 46, 50
Stein, Stephen, 5, 13, 18, 21, 97
Steinmetz, David, 19
Stiles, Ezra, 2
Stoddard, Solomon, 25, 27, 29, 33, 84
Storms, Samuel, 81
Stout, Harry, 90
Sweeney, Douglas, 4–5, 7–10, 12, 19, 21–22, 75–76, 109

Theusen, Peter, 21
Thompson, John, 18
Tracy, Patricia, 46, 51
Turretin, Francis, 81, 100, 102–3, 111

Valeri, Mark, 30, 86
VanDoodewaard, William, 13, 79–80
Vlastuin, Willem van, 80

Watts, Isaac, 96
Westerhoff, Benjamin, 10–11
Westra, Helen, 1, 3
Whitby, Daniel, 96
Wilkins, John, 26
Williams, William, 33
Wilson, John, 64–65

Yoo, Jeongmo, 13

Scripture Index

Genesis
1–3	79–80, 90
1:26–29	93, 100–101
1:26	96–97, 102
1:27	27, 93–97
3	30, 56, 74
3:17–19	27
3:4	27
3:11	55–56, 63, 68, 75
3:15	56, 62, 67–68
3:24	29–30, 60
4	35
4:3–5	27
4:1	62, 68
4:7	33, 40
4:26	68
6:1–2	68
6:22	27
9:6	95–96
12:2	46–47, 51, 55, 63, 108
12:3	27
12:12	70
14	69
15	69–70
15:1	27
15:11	69
19:14	27, 29
19:17	27
22	69
24:58	27
25:29–34	27
27:39	27
28	63
28:12	42–43, 70, 108
32	40, 51
32:24–32	27
32:26–29	33, 35
37–50	71
39	51
39:12	50, 108
41:45	72
43:3	27, 71
45:20	72
49:8–9	73

Deuteronomy
22:8	53

Judges
16:10	27

Psalm
89:6	82

Scripture Index

Proverbs
8:27–31	100
22:1	48
28:26	52

Ecclesiastes
3:4	55

Isaiah
6:8	100
9:6	100
40:13–14	100
49:3	43
51:8	64–66

Ezekiel
20:21–22	46

Matthew
5:27–28	53
5:45	48
7:14	45
15:21–23	37–39

Mark
10:46–48	39

Luke
11:5	37
18	37
22:32	89

John
1:1–4	100
1:51	43
5:17–19	100
16:8	97
17:21–22	100

Acts
20:35	48

1 Corinthians
1:29–31	87
2:10–11	100
2:14	105
15:28	60

2 Corinthians
4	82, 105

Ephesians
4:24	100

Colossians
3:10	100

Hebrews
1:14	45
5:12	20
11:17–19	70
11:4	33
11:8	47

1 Peter
1:8	91

2 Peter
1:4	88
2:7–8	27

1 John
3:6	105

3 John
11	105

Jude
23	53

Revelation
14:13	42

www.ingramcontent.com/pod-product-compliance
Lightning Source LLC
Chambersburg PA
CBHW071623170426
43195CB00038B/2049